Saving & Investing

Saving & Investing

*How to achieve financial security
and make your money grow*

JOHN WHITELEY
3rd edition

How To Books

Published by How To Books Ltd,
3 Newtec Place, Magdalen Road,
Oxford OX4 1RE. United Kingdom.
Tel: (01865) 793806. Fax: (01865) 248780.
email: info@howtobooks.co.uk
http://www.howtobooks.co.uk

Third edition 2000

British Library Cataloguing in Publication Data.
A catalogue record for this book is available from
the British Library.

Cartoons by Mike Flanagan
Cover design by Shireen Nathoo Design
Cover image PhotoDisc
Cover copy by Sallyann Sheridan

Produced for How To Books by Deer Park Productions
Typeset by Concept Communications (Design & Print) Ltd,
Crayford, Kent
Printed and bound by Cromwell Press, Trowbridge, Wiltshire

NOTE: The material contained in this book is set out in good
faith for general guidance and no liability can be accepted
for loss or expense incurred as a result of relying in particular
circumstances on statements made in the book. Laws and
regulations are complex and liable to change, and readers should
check the current position with the relevant authorities before
making personal arrangements.

Contents

List of illustrations

Preface

If you feel that savings and investments are too complicated, too full of jargon, and surrounded by a mystique, then this is the book for you. I have tried to de-mystify the subject, and explain it in plain English. I have set out a few simple guidelines, and scattered throughout the book are my 'Twelve Commandments' of saving and investing.

This book is for ordinary people who want to be in control of their own financial destiny. It was born out of a conviction that ordinary people can successfully implement their own saving and investment strategy. All that is needed is an understanding of the basic principles.

This book does **not** promise to make you rich overnight. What it does is to guide you through what can seem like a jungle by keeping in mind your objectives – and prompting you to keep your objectives under regular review.

In my work as a chartered accountant in public practice, I met people from many walks of life, and of varying degrees of wealth. I have drawn on over 20 years of experience to help you in this book.

John Whiteley

1

Defining Your Objectives

WHAT DO YOU WANT TO DO?

If you aim for nothing, you will probably hit it. Many people feel they would like to save or invest, but it remains a vague feeling. They may succeed in putting aside some money in a savings account of some sort, but it goes no further. They have no purpose or aim in their saving. The savings they have might be a nice little nest egg, but if it has no direct purpose, it can too easily get used up in the first emergency, or even the first whim, that comes along.

Make it your first task to sit down and think about your aims. This will help you to structure your savings and investments. For example, if you want to save for your retirement, you will want to put your savings in a place where you cannot touch them until your retirement date. Otherwise, you might be tempted to use the money for something else, and then find yourself short when you come to retire.

Here are some of the most common aims for saving:

- generating an income

- protecting your capital

- combating inflation

- providing for your retirement

- passing on your wealth to the next generation

- putting a deposit on a house

- paying for education of your children or grandchildren

- having the holiday of a lifetime

- buying an expensive item such as a boat

- replacing a car.

CHANGING YOUR OBJECTIVES

It is evident that you may well have a different set of objectives at different points of your life. As a young person, you may want to save up for that flashy sports car, or the latest in windsurfing gear. Then you settle into married life, and you want to buy a house, or trade up to a better house. Children come along, and you think about their education. In middle life, you are more and more concerned about approaching retirement, and how to provide for that. At last you retire, and now you want to supplement your income from your savings. Some years into retirement, you may think about passing on your wealth to your successors.

At all times, be aware of your changing circumstances, and plan your savings with them in mind. Changes usually happen slowly, and we do not always recognise them. Therefore, take time every so often – say every five years – to review where your life is and where it is going. Then make any changes necessary to your saving habits.

The twelve commandments of saving and investing
As we go through this book, we will look at these twelve commandments. The first is –

Keep it simple.

In all your plans for savings and investments, try not to complicate matters any more than need be. This will help your flexibility.

GENERATING AN INCOME

If you tried to live on the basic state pension, you might find it difficult. Many people use their accumulated savings to generate income, to supplement the basic pension. If this is your aim, then invest your savings in a form which will generate this income for you.

It is always wise to bear in mind the effect of inflation, so try to obtain from your savings an income that has at least the possibility of escalating year by year, particularly if you have no other means of earning.

PROTECTING YOUR CAPITAL AND COMBATING INFLATION

These two are really the same objective. If inflation is high, the real value of your savings gets eroded. For example, if inflation is at ten per cent per year, your money will buy ten per cent less next year than it bought this year. This has only to continue for five years for your money to be halved in value.

This is bad enough when applied to income, but even worse when you consider the effect on your savings. This effect is particularly relevant in planning for retirement. You are wise to start saving for retirement as early as possible. Therefore, you could start saving when your retirement is 30 or even 40 years away. Even with fairly low rates of inflation – less then five per cent – your savings would be severely eroded in 30 or 40 years' time. Therefore your main objective would be to save in a form that protects your savings against inflation.

Having your cake and eating it

You may decide that you would like the best of both worlds. You would like an income from your savings but you would also like to protect the capital. Certain types of investment purport to do that. However, they inevitably represent a compromise of some kind.

A **pure growth** type of investment will not provide much of an income, if any. A **pure income** type of investment will not usually be outstanding for its capital growth. An investment which tries to provide both aspects is usually a split investment of some kind. Half the investment is put into a growth type investment and the other half in an income type investment. The income is halved and the growth potential is halved.

This leads us to the next two Commandments of Saving and Investing:

> You cannot buck the market, so do not try to.
> If something seems too good to be true, it probably is.

These two rules are really different ways of saying the same thing. In saying that you cannot buck the market, you recognise that the law of supply and demand has created certain rates of return on different types of savings and investments. There will always be variations within a certain range. For example, shares in companies in the same sector (say, insurance companies) will offer a similar return.

However, if any one investment in a certain field offers a rate of return which is significantly out of step with others in the same field, there is usually a significant risk element attached.

USING YOUR CRYSTAL BALL

Unless you are endowed with second sight, you do not know what the future holds. One in three marriages ends in divorce, and a divorce can seriously upset the best planned savings and investment strategy.

Divorce may be the most obvious wild card in the pack, but many other things can cause your plans to go awry — redundancy, ill health, *etc.*

It is always a good idea, therefore, to try to make your savings as flexible as possible. Ask questions about any investment you undertake, such as:

● Can I unscramble it if necessary?

● Is it readily encashable?

● Is the value liable to fall as well as rise?

● Can I pass it on easily to my descendants?

PLANNING BEYOND THE GRAVE

One consideration which may loom large in your thinking is how to pass your savings on to the next generation. Or perhaps you may have a favourite charity which you would like to benefit after your death.

If these are your concerns, then you need to consider another dimension to planning your savings. That is, of course, minimising Inheritance Tax.

Ordering your priorities

As valid as these concerns may be, they should be kept in perspective. Do not jeopardise your present plans for the sake of passing on the most you can. Make sure that you are adequately provided for in the here and now.

CHECKLIST

● Sort out your aims. Write them down.

● Review your aims regularly.

● Know what to do if
  – you want to generate income, or
  – you want to protect your capital, or
  – you want to do both.

● Be ready to change and try to keep your investments flexible.

● Do not fall for anything if it seems too good to be true.

CASE STUDIES

Through this book, we will be looking at a number of situations in which people find themselves at various stages of life. Here is an introduction to some of the characters we shall meet.

Alison

Alison graduated from university a couple of years ago. She lives in a rented flat, and has just become engaged to be married. She and her fiancé are saving to buy their first house, and they are both trying to make a career for themselves. They do not plan to start a family yet. Alison's present savings aim is to save enough for a deposit on a house, then to be able to pay the mortgage. She is not thinking any further ahead than that. Her fiancé, however, has been talking to others, and wants her to think about planning further ahead, and to start a pension plan.

Brian

Brian is in his late 40s, has a good job, is married and has two children. One has just married, the other is at university. For the first time in his life, he is now able to save regularly. He worries whether he has enough saved up for his retirement.

His wife has recently taken a part time job, and likes to have some money she can call her own.

Charles

Charles is married and has just retired. He has a company pension, and a life assurance endowment policy is due to mature. His wife is a few years younger than him, and she wants to continue working for the time being. Charles does not yet have any positive ideas about what to do with his endowment. He has not yet budgeted for living in retirement, and has a vague idea that, with his company pension and the state pension, he will manage, although he realises that he will not be as well off as before. He always had it in mind that he and his wife would take a cruise when he retired.

A friend takes him aside and tells him he must plan his lifestyle in retirement, and plan his finances as well. He starts to take this seriously, and when the endowment matures, decides to put it for the time being into a building society account which gives him good interest, but where he can realise his money without undue delay.

POINTS TO CONSIDER

1. Do you know what you expect to achieve from your savings? How can you make a working plan to help you achieve your goals?

2. Do you have an idea of where you are going in your life? How can the savings plan be tailored to fit your plans?

3. How can you plan to cope with uncertainties and unexpected calamities?

2

Understanding the Environment

KNOWING WHAT YOU ARE GETTING YOURSELF INTO

It is helpful to know the background to financial and economic life, because that is what your savings and investments are going into. Here then is a brief history of commerce and finance. If you have a degree in economics, you may skip this part.

In the beginning, people lived in small groups of hunters and gatherers. They hunted animals for meat, and gathered fruit, berries and grains. Then they began to cultivate the land. Their dwellings had to become more permanent, and they developed skills at making things – using tools. Before long, they realised that they would need to specialise. Instead of one person making all his requirements, he would do better to specialise in making one thing or group of things, and other people specialised in making other things.

For this system to work, there had to be a method of trading one thing for another. How could you decide what, say, a pig was worth? Five sacks of grain? Six knives? Or would five pigs buy you a cart? It was like having a set of scales, with different items on each side, and trying to balance the scales.

Money – the big idea

Then someone had the idea of putting something (let us call it money) in the middle, so that everything could be measured by reference to this 'money'. Thus, for instance, one pig would be worth, say, ten 'moneys'. A sack of grain might be worth two 'moneys', and a cart might be worth 50 'moneys'. Money became the means of exchanging things, and also the means of measuring the worth of things. For our purposes, we can make a good case for saying that money was the most important invention of the human race, enabling it to develop commercially.

But then, money itself had to take on some permanent form, and one that everyone recognised and accepted. As skills and technologies increased, it would be no good for a farmer from one county selling pigs or sheep for money – which to him was sea shells – and then trying to buy farm implements in another county, where their money was precious stones. So money became standardised in the form of precious metals – predominantly gold.

The development of banking

As people's skills developed, trades and industries sprang up. With this, it became more difficult to keep and carry around all the money people needed. So certain people – let us call them bankers – agreed to keep people's money, and give them receipts for the money. These receipts themselves were then used as money, and became bank notes.

In time, the bankers realised that not everybody wanted their money at once. In fact, it soon became obvious that, at any one time, only a small proportion of people would want their money. So they used the excess money to lend to people who needed it. In return, the people who borrowed the money paid back a little more than they borrowed – this was called 'interest'. Soon, the practice of lending money on interest became a vital part of commerce.

Many banks sprang up in different parts of the country, but the constraints of modern finance have led to mergers, and banks becoming bigger and bigger.

A particular form of lending is the lending of money to people to buy their homes. Mutual societies grew up around the turn of the last century, known as building societies. These took money from a large number of people saving money with them and loaned money to a smaller number of people to buy houses. Many of these have recently 'demutualised' and become banks, but their core business remains the same.

The formation of companies

Then people realised that businesses were becoming too big to manage single-handed. So they formed partnerships so that several people could work together to manage a business. The idea grew that some people could participate in a business by putting money into it, but not actually take part in the management. So companies came into existence, where people could become shareholders in the company, while leaving the management to others. This separation of ownership from management remains to this day as a principle of limited companies.

The concept of limited liability came along to further encourage business development. This means that a limited company has a separate legal existence from its owners. So, if a company failed and owed money, the owners (*ie* the shareholders) could not lose any more than the money they had already put in the business.

The evolution of shares

As companies and investors got more sophisticated, the pattern of share-holding was refined. Shares became divided into different classes. Nowadays there are typically **ordinary shares** and **preference shares**.

Ordinary shares

These remain the main form of investing in a company. Holding shares means that you own part of the company and you take the risks of the business. Your reward is a share in the company's profits. This is called the **dividend**. Therefore, the reward you get each year will not be the same. If a business is growing, and making extra profits, you will get extra dividends each year.

Ordinary shareholders, however, are the last to be paid out in case of failure. This is the risk element.

Dividends and earnings

Dividends are the amounts paid to the shareholders from the company's profits. However, not all of the profits are distributed to shareholders. Some of the profits may need to be kept back for investment in new equipment, *etc.*

A common measure of performance of a company is **earnings per share**. This is basically the profit of the company divided by the number of shares in issue. This is not the same as dividend per share, for the reason outlined above. This gives rise to another measure known as **dividend cover**. This is the difference between the earnings per share and the dividend per share. If the difference is small, there is said to be low dividend cover.

For instance, if a company made earnings per share of £1.20, and paid a dividend of £1 per share, the dividend cover is 1.2 times. This is an important measure, since it shows how vulnerable the dividends would be from this company. If the dividend cover is low, and the company went on to make a reduced profit the next year, the dividend would be likely to fall substantially. If, however, the dividend cover was high, there would be more in reserve. This means that a fall in the profit level would not necessarily lead to a fall in the dividend.

Thus, if the earnings per share were £2, and the dividend paid were £1, the dividend cover is 2 times. Then, if the company's profit dropped by 25 per cent, its earnings per share would then be £1.50. It would still be able to pay a dividend of £1 per share.

Preference shares

Preference shares are, as the name implies, preferred over ordinary shares in the case of failure. If you held preference shares in a company that went bust, you would get paid out before the ordinary shareholders.

However, preference shareholders receive a fixed rate of interest on their shares, not a share in the profits.

Convertible preference shares

A fairly recent development has been the issue of convertible preference shares. These are preference shares which give fixed interest only, and which share the preferred status, but which also give the right to convert them at some future date into ordinary shares of the company, usually at a fixed price.

Warrants

Warrants are a further refinement. They are usually issued to ordinary shareholders as a form of incentive. They give the shareholder the right to buy further shares at a future date at a fixed price. These warrants themselves can be sold to another person, and so represent a valuable bonus.

Other types of investment

Loan capital

Apart from holders of shares, other people can invest in companies by lending the company money. This is done by means of **debentures** or **loan stocks**. These are in some ways similar to preference shares – they pay a fixed rate of interest, and they may be bought and sold. But unlike preference shares, the holder of a debenture or loan stock is not a part owner of the company.

Government stocks

You can also become an investor in your country by buying government stocks. In practically all countries, the governments do not raise enough in taxes to pay for all they have to. They have to raise other money by borrowing from people. These government stocks are also known as **gilts** because they are reckoned as being 'as safe as the Bank of England'. That is because they are ultimately guaranteed by the Bank of England. To do this, the government has to pay interest, and government stocks are shown as, for example '8% Treasury Stock 2002'. This indicates that the stock pays interest at 8 per cent per annum, and is repayable in the year 2002.

Building societies and banks

As described above, banks came into being as a means of facilitating trade. They were therefore an integral part of the economic development of this or any other country. They also developed the personal banking side to their activities, and now of course, there are not many people who have not opened a bank account of one sort or another.

Building societies are also mentioned above. These remained for a long time as simple mutual societies which gave savers a fair rate of interest, and charged borrowers a fair rate of interest to buy their houses.

A relatively recent development, however, saw banks and building societies encroaching more and more on each others' domains. This has led in the recent past to several larger building societies demutualising and becoming banks.

CASE STUDIES

Alison has a working knowledge of economics

Alison studied economics, and has a good grasp of how the economy works. Her decisions will be based on this understanding.

Brian will rely on professionals

Brian does not have an in-depth understanding of the subtle differences between shares, unit trusts, government stocks *etc*. He intends to rely on professional advice when making his investment decisions.

Charles wants to know more

Charles likes to investigate and read up on anything he undertakes. He will find out as much as he can about anything he puts his money into.

POINTS TO CONSIDER

1. Do you think it is really necessary to understand all the intricacies of the economy and financial matters before you make your decisions about money?

2. How far do you think you should put your trust in professional advisers?

3

Evaluating the Risk/Reward Relationship

Here is the fourth Commandment of Saving and Investing:

> There is no reward without risk

UNDERSTANDING THE RISKS

When making your plans for savings and investments, you must decide about the degree of risk you are happy with. This does not mean that your degree of risk is set in concrete. You may change your attitude to risk at different times of your life, or depending on how much money you have to invest. Remember one of the first principles in this book: review your circumstances regularly (and this includes a changing attitude to risk) and be ready to change your savings plan if necessary.

Beware of 'guaranteed'

Many investments are marketed on advertising which promotes the safety aspect. Any such advertisements are targeted at what are known as 'risk averse investors'. You may see the word 'guaranteed' feature in advertisements or in the name of the product. Beware of this word! Find out all you can about the investment before committing your money. In particular, read the small print to find out exactly what is guaranteed.

Another advertisement I saw recently read as follows:
'Penny Shares are booming. Make an average gain of 354% on shares costing less than £1'. The risk warning appeared further down the advertisement, in much smaller print. This was an advertisement for a 'tip sheet' giving tips for investing in shares of small companies. The shares are of low value, under £1. Therefore, an increase in the price of one of these shares by, say 10 pence each, will be a much greater potential to make larger gains on this type of investment. Because of the nature of it, however, there is also the potential to make larger losses.

JUDGING THE RISK PROFILE

There are some obvious pointers to the risk profile.

Assessing the quality of information

If you get chatting to a fellow at the pub, whom you only know by sight, and he recommends a sure-fire tip for the 2.30 at Newmarket, you would not put all your savings on it. If that same fellow offered to sell you some shares in a gold-prospecting company which had just found gold in the wilds of Alaska, your reaction would probably be the same.

Your assessment of the risk is coloured by your judgement of the quality of the information. One of the main factors in this is the trust and confidence you have in the person giving you the information.

Here is the fifth Commandment of Saving and Investing:

You cannot have too much information.

However, information always comes from someone. It may be the man in the pub, or the pages of the *Financial Times*, or anywhere in between those two extremes.

If you are at all uncertain, try to corroborate the information with someone in whom you have confidence.

What is behind it?

All forms of saving and investment have something behind them. Take, for instance, a building society account. By saving in this you are putting money into a large pool which is then loaned to people buying a house. That is very simple to understand, and very 'transparent'. You can see easily that the ultimate investment of the money is in bricks and mortar.

Other forms of investment may not be quite so transparent. A name such as 'General Amalgamated Consolidated Portfolio PLC' does not really give any clue as to what your money would be invested in. So always make a point of trying to find out what is behind it. Is it a chain of seedy night-clubs? Is it an international group exploiting the resources of the third world?

You may be considering investing in a **unit trust** or **investment trust**. As we shall see in a later chapter, these work on the principle of spreading the risk. They put money from small investors into a large fund, which is then spread in a wide variety of companies. But you then need to look further into it. Many unit trusts specialise in certain types of company or investment, or certain geographical areas. For instance, a trust labelled as **high income** or **high yield** will probably have all or a large part of its investments in fixed interest government stocks, or other fixed interest investments. A **growth** trust will probably be invested to a large extent in smaller companies judged to have potential for growth.

How big is it?

A further indicator of risk is the size of the company or fund into which you are investing. Taking the example of the unit trust again, look at the literature. What is the size of the fund? Is it several millions? Or is it tens of millions? Or for a company, what is the total market value of all the shares in issue? (This is known as the market capitalisation.)

When you know how big the fund or company is, you can make your own decisions. This is one area where big may be beautiful, but smaller companies or funds often provide better performance.

How marketable is it?

Another factor in judging the degree of risk attaching to a particular investment is the extent of marketability. The ultimate in marketability for company shares is, of course, the Stock Exchange. In order to qualify to be traded on the Stock Exchange, a company must meet stringent requirements. Anybody owning shares in those companies may sell them openly to any other willing buyer. The number of transactions on the Stock Exchange runs into millions every week.

At the other end of the scale could be a small family company. The shares may be owned by, say, mother, father and two sons. If one of them wanted to sell their shares, the rules of the company may dictate that they can only sell them to directors of the company. Even if this rule did not exist, it would not be easy to find a buyer outside the family willing to buy shares in that company.

In general terms, shares in smaller companies are not so marketable as shares in bigger companies.

Timing

If the investment is dated, or has a fixed redemption date, then there is a higher risk attached to it. That is because you must take the capital proceeds when it matures. That might not be a propitious time for re-investment. On the other hand, if an investment is open ended, then it can be cashed in to suit your circumstances, and is therefore less risky.

LOW RISK INVESTMENTS

Playing safe

It is obvious that the opposite indicators to high risk investments attach to low risk investments. In summary, these are:

- The higher the quality of information, the lower risk there will be.

- The more transparent the investment, the lower the risk.

- The larger the company or trust, the lower the risk.

- The more marketable the investment, the lower the risk.

- Dated investments are more risky than open ended ones.

It is therefore obvious that putting your money into some form of government backed investment (either government stocks or National Savings) has the lowest risk profile. It may also appear that putting money into something like a bank or building society deposit account is also a low risk profile. However, you must bear in mind that if your money is in an interest bearing account, the capital is static, and is eroded by inflation.

Short term and long term risk

Therefore, it could be said that a deposit account is a low risk profile in the short term, but a high risk profile in the long term. To take it further, the higher the rate of inflation, the higher the long term risk profile. Conversely, an equity-based investment has the prospect of keeping up with inflation. It could therefore be said to have a higher short term risk profile, but a lower long term risk profile.

PUTTING YOUR EGGS IN DIFFERENT BASKETS

The old adage holds good in investment matters. Within the limitations of your available money, try not to put all your eggs in one basket. Try to have a mix of equity based and fixed interest investment. Range your investments from ultra-safe to the highest risk you are happy with.

If you do not have enough money for a range of equity investments, then limit your exposure to this sector to unit trust or investment trust companies (see Chapter 6).

THE RISK/REWARD RELATIONSHIP

Remember the fourth Commandment? – **There is no reward without risk.**

What this means is that if your expect a reward of some sort, no matter how modest, there has to be some element of risk attached. What you want to do is to minimise the risk factor as far as possible while not affecting your reward too seriously. The general relationship remains as an overall rule of thumb, which can be expressed as:

Low risk profile = low reward

High risk profile = high reward.

CHECKLIST

Evaluate your risk exposure, and decide how far you are willing to go on risk exposure. Factors of risk:

- quality of information
- transparency
- size
- marketability
- timing.

CASE STUDIES

Alison goes for low risk

Although Alison has a good understanding of financial matters, she is at the start of her career, and starting to save to buy a house. She is happy at present to keep a low risk profile, and to limit her savings to the things that will enable her to achieve her immediate goals. However, she does start to put something away into a pension scheme.

Brian exercises caution

Brian is mainly worried about retirement, and also wants to keep a low risk profile. However, this is because he has not had any experience of serious investing previously. He is willing to take advice.

Charles doesn't mind a degree of risk

Charles has had no formal education in financial matters, but will find out everything he can, and take advice. He is willing to commit part of his money to investments which have a certain degree of risk attached.

POINTS TO CONSIDER

1. How will you decide your risk exposure?

2. Will your risk decision be affected by

   – the income you are looking to generate

   – the size of your available capital?

3. Can you foresee circumstances in which you might be willing to revise your risk exposure? If so, would it mean any great upheaval in your savings and investments?

4

Structuring Your Savings

Before actually committing any of your money, you should have a clear idea in your mind of how your savings are to be structured. This will largely depend on your objectives, which you should already have determined by this time.

Structure is a little different from **objective**. It concerns the detailed planning of how you intend to achieve your objective.

KEEPING READY MONEY

It is always necessary, of course, to keep enough money in a form which allows you to live from one day, or week, to the next. This may seem obvious, but you must not let your current 'living' money run out. This ready money may be in several forms. Most people keep a few pounds in their pocket or purse at all times. You may also have money that you keep in the house. For obvious reasons, it is not recommended to keep very much in this form. A current account at the bank is perhaps the most common way to keep this ready money. Some of these accounts give interest on the running balance, but the interest rate is usually so low that it is not a real incentive.

An overdraft facility at the bank is also, effectively, a part of your ready cash. However, it should only be used to iron out any troughs and peaks in your cash flow. If you use it on a permanent basis, it is an expensive way of being able to have ready cash. Some businesses may have to run almost permanently on an overdraft, but try not to let that become a permanent feature of your personal finances.

Building societies (including those that have recently demutualised) have instant access accounts which operate on a similar basis to bank current accounts. Many of them offer cheque book and cash card facilities. Others operate on a pass-book basis. This means that you have to go to the building society to draw out your money when you need it. Some people are happier with this type of account.

Rainy day money

As well as ready money, it is a good idea to keep some money in an account which you can access fairly easily – say, with a week's notice, or at most a month. This money is to cope with emergencies. Your roof, or your car, might need an urgent repair. Or you might want to help out a member of your family with an urgent need. A rainy day fund is indispensable for this sort of thing. The actual amount to keep in the rainy day account is a personal matter for you. Of course you never know how much you might need to lay your hands on immediately, but decide on a figure, then find the best home you can for it – *ie* the one that gives the best combination of interest and access.

You may have a situation where you know that a certain amount will be payable, and you know when it will be payable. In this case, you can safely put it in an account which needs a long period of notice – or even a fixed term account. Just as long as it is available on the date you need it.

INVESTING LONG TERM

The main part of your money should go to achieving your objectives. Thus, if you decide your main objective is to generate income, most of your money should go into an investment which will produce the best income for you. If you decide you would also like to try to protect your capital, then you must decide what proportion of your money you will invest in investments to provide capital growth. The actual proportion depends on

- how much you have to invest and

- what degree of importance you attach to income generation and capital protection.

PLAYING WITH MONEY

If you have enough, and if you are so inclined, you may set aside a small part of your money to play with. If you think you would like to speculate on the stock market, or with any other form of speculative investment, then set aside a relatively small part of your money to indulge this habit. But always realise that this is high risk money, and you must be prepared for the eventuality that you lose it all.

SAVING REGULARLY

Some savings and investment products can be made by a lump sum.

Others can be made only by regular monthly savings. Some may be done in either way. Decide how much capital you have to invest as a lump sum, and how much you want to save regularly. This will also be part of your overall structure.

Pound cost averaging

Regular monthly investing in unit trusts or investment trusts can be advantageous when the market is fluctuating. An annual investment carries more risk of catching the market at the wrong time. Monthly investment means that any fluctuations are ironed out.

SPREADING IT ABOUT

Once you have decided on the outline of your structure, it is time to put some flesh on the bones. Once again, the principle of not putting all your eggs in one basket comes into play. This time, it is not only to spread the risk. You also want to spread your money about to try to achieve your objective in the best way. If, for example, you put the whole of your money to generate an income into one unit trust, the dividends, although good, would probably only be paid twice a year (although some do pay quarterly). This may cause cash flow problems. Spreading it about into, say, four or five unit trusts would mean that there is more of a flow of income through the year.

The sixth commandment of saving and investing

Whatever structure you decide on, always bear in mind this commandment:

Do not try to live off your capital.

CHECKLIST

● Decide on your main objective.

● Decide how much you will devote to that.

● Keep aside some ready money and rainy day money.

● Decide how much will be saved regularly.

● Then, if you wish, have some 'play money'.

CASE STUDIES

Alison saves for a house

Alison knows she must save hard for the deposit on buying a house. She therefore finds the best interest rate on offer for 'regular savings' – *ie* monthly savings. She is also putting aside a modest amount in a pension plan.

Brian saves for his retirement

Brian decides his main aim is to save for his retirement. He puts away as much as he can into a pension plan. He also has a legacy from a distant relative which he would like to invest. He does not particularly want extra income now, but would like to see the lump sum grow until he retires, then he would start to use it for income generation. He has a building society account with £3,000 in it. He would like to see a little more in this for his 'rainy day' money, but decides he must concentrate more on his main objective.

Charles spreads his risks

Charles has the endowment proceeds in a building society account at present, and this totals over £40,000. He wants to invest it mainly to generate extra income, but the more he reads, the more he is willing to speculate with some of his money. After talking to his wife, he decides to leave £5,000 in the building society, invest £30,000 for income generation, and put the rest in a higher risk investment, which he could monitor regularly, and if needs be, change from time to time.

POINTS TO CONSIDER

1. Have you done an 'inventory' of all your assets?

2. How will you decide what proportion to dedicate to your main aim?

3. How will you decide how much to keep aside as 'rainy day' money?

4. How will you know if you are trying to live off your capital?

5

Tackling the Stock Market

DEALING IN STOCKS AND SHARES

The Stock Exchanges of the world were set up to provide a marketplace for those wishing to buy or sell shares. The growth of limited liability companies produced a need for shareholders to be able to buy or sell shares. Without this facility, far fewer people would have been willing to invest in companies. For the purposes of this book, we are looking at the way the London Stock Exchange works.

To trade in shares, you need to deal through a **stockbroker**. The stockbroker deals on the Stock Exchange through **market shares**, or through the **SETS trading system** on the London Stock Exchange.

Market makers

Market makers are traders who deal only with brokers. If a broker approaches a market maker stating that he wants to deal in a certain quantity of a particular share, the market maker will quote two prices – one at which he will offer to buy, the other at which he will offer to sell. The difference between the buying price and the selling price is called the spread. If the broker is satisfied, he will then tell the market maker whether he wants to buy or sell, and the quantity.

SETS

At the time of writing, the SETS system has just been started on the London Stock Exchange, but only for dealing in shares in the top 100 shares. This is a computer system which displays offers for sale and offers for purchase with the quantities on offer for each share in the top 100. The computer then matches up the buyers and sellers.

Settling the bills

When a deal has been made, the stockbroker will send you an account. This shows the number of shares dealt, the price of dealing, and any expenses such as stamp duty and their own commission. See Figure 1.

Settlement is five working days afterwards. If you have bought, the

Laing & Cruickshank Investment Management Ltd

Member of The London Stock Exchange
Regulated by The Securities & Futures Authority
Member of The Credit Lyonnais Group

BROADWALK HOUSE 5 APPOLD STREET LONDON EC2A 2DA
TELEPHONE 0171-588 2800 TELEX 9419248 LACIM FAX 0171-374 0066 DX 699 LONDON/CITY

Contract Note/Advice Note

SUBJECT TO THE RULES AND REGULATIONS OF THE LONDON STOCK EXCHANGE

WE HAVE AS AGENTS SOLD BY ORDER AND FOR THE ACCOUNT OF

ON 23 FEB 98 (TAX POINT) AT 4.01PM

***** FOR SETTLEMENT ON 02 MAR 98 *****

866 BRITISH TELECOMMUNICATIONS
ORD 25P

```
          @ £ 5.995                                    £        5,191.67
                                      LESS
   £5,191.67 @  1.85%  =      96.05   CONTRACT FEE      £           25.00
                                      COMMISSION        £           96.05
                                      VAT
                                      EXEMPT            £            0.00
                                                              -----------------
                                      TOTAL CREDIT      £        5,070.62
                                                              =================
```

****
TO ENSURE PROMPT SETTLEMENT PLEASE SEND US THE RELEVANT DOCUMENTS. WE
RESERVE THE RIGHT TO RECOUP ANY COSTS INCURRED THROUGH LATE DELIVERY.
****

```
                              BARGAIN NO.  QBO0499B00
                              52026C /76  (0-140-843)


                              DUPLICATE COPY
```

E&OE

Registered in England No1325665
Registered Office: - as above
VAT No. 647 2599 17

Fig. 1. Contract note from stockbroker.

Laing & Cruickshank Investment Management Ltd

Registered in England No 1325565
Registered Office Broadwalk House,
5 Appold St, London EC2A 2DA

VAT Regn No 447 2599 17

Member of The London Stock Exchange
Regulated by The Securities & Futures Authority
Member of The Credit Lyonnais Group

Broadwalk House
5, Appold Street
London EC2A 2DA

Telephone 0171-588 2800
Facsimile 0171-374 0066
DX 699 London/City

Statement of Account
Period To   13/03/98

Ref.

Page   1

RE ACCOUNT :

Date	Transaction	Debit	Credit
	Pounds Sterling Brought Forward Balance	£ 0.00	
	Current Statement Period Transactions		
17/02/98	BGHT 800 BRITISH PETROLEUM CO ORD 25P QBH0273B00 @ £ 7.935 EX-DIV Value date 03/03/98	£ 6,522.18	
17/02/98	BGHT 6300 AMEC 6.5P (NET) CUM CNV PRF 50P QBH0279B00 @ £ 0.98 Value date 03/03/98	£ 6,344.09	
17/02/98	SOLD 2600 FLEMING AMERICAN INVESTMENT TRUST 7½ CNV UNS LN STK 1999 QBH0284B00 @ £ 505 Value date 03/03/98		£ 12,904.10
	Balance as at 13/03/98		£ 37.83

E&OE

Fig. 2. Statement from stockbroker.

amount is payable to your stockbroker. If you have sold, the stockbroker will pay you. You may, of course, have sold one shareholding and bought another. In this case, all transactions on the same day will be aggregated and the net amount will be due from you or to you. See Figure 2.

CHOOSING AND USING A STOCKBROKER

Finding a stockbroker who will take you on as a client is not too difficult. They are in business, and they will not turn away the right sort of client. The best introduction to a stockbroker is through a friend or relation who is already a client. They will be able to tell you how good they feel the service is. Alternatively, a professional adviser such as an accountant or solicitor can probably recommend a stockbroker to you.

Once you have a stockbroker, stay with him or her unless there is some serious problem. The relationship you build up over the years will prove very useful. The service you get from your stockbroker will be one of:

- advisory

- execution only

- discretionary.

Advisory
This means that the stockbroker advises you either when you request advice on, say, whether to sell, or on investing a lump sum, or when he or she feels that a particular purchase or sale would be a good move.

Execution only
This means that the stockbroker will make a certain deal for you, simply on your instructions. They may have no opinion, or they may advise against it, but if you still give the order to go ahead, they carry out your request.

Discretionary
This means that you give the stockbroker the right to manage your shares. The stockbroker will hold your shares in a nominee company, in an account that is designated in your name. They will then go ahead and make any deals which they consider to be right for you.

HAVING YOUR PORTFOLIO MANAGED

A stockbroker will normally take on a portfolio of shares provided that it is of a reasonable size. At present, this would probably mean a minimum of £50,000. He or she would then load the details on the computer, and provide you with a valuation list. This would then be updated and sent to you periodically, typically once or twice a year. Figure 3 shows what a typical valuation statement looks like.

Understanding a valuation statement
The valuation statement gives the following information:

- Summary of investments by sector. This shows the total value broken down into the different sectors of the economy.

- Geographical analysis. This shows how the investments are spread through the world.

- Individual details. This shows each investment separately, and gives the following details:
  - Holding. This means the number of shares of each type.
  - Market price. This is the price of the share at the date of the valuation.
  - Market value. This is the total value of the shares, obtained by multiplying the holding by the market price.
  - Book cost. This is the actual price at which you bought the investment. By comparing this with the market value, you can see whether you are currently showing a profit or a loss.
  - Dividend rate. This is the latest declared dividend rate of the company, and is expressed in money terms per share.
  - Estimated gross income. This is the dividend rate multiplied by the number of shares. It shows you how much you should receive in the current year from the investment.
  - Dividend yield. This is the income expressed as a percentage of the market value. It means that if you bought that investment at the market price on the day of the valuation, the actual income as a percentage of the price is different from the dividend rate. This is called the yield and is the only safe measure of comparing one investment with another.
  - Dividends due. This tells you when the forthcoming dividends are likely to be paid. There are usually two dividends payments in a year, although some companies pay four dividends in a year.

Laing & Cruickshank Investment Management Ltd

Member of The London Stock Exchange
Regulated by The Securities & Futures Authority
Member of the Credit Lyonnais Group

Portfolio Valuation

Security description	Holding	Market price	Market value	Book cost	Dividend rate	Estimated Gross income	%Div. yield	Dividends Due
FIXED INTEREST								
UNITED KINGDOM								
FIXED INTEREST/CONVERTIBLES								
BRITISH FUNDS								
EXCHEQUER 9 3/4% STK 1998	£ 7,051.23	£ 101 34 days	£ 7,122 £ 64	£ 6,433	9.75%	£ 687	9.65	Jan Jul
CONVERSION 9% STK 2000	£ 6,501.63	£ 104 3/16 172 days XD	£ 6,774 £ 276	£ 6,298	9.00%	£ 585	8.64	Mar Sep
TREASURY 8% STK 2003	£ 14,494.29	£ 104 1/8 73 days	£ 15,092 £ 232	£ 14,502	8.00%	£ 1,160	7.68	Jun Dec
TREASURY 8% LN 2002/06	£ 6,484.22	£ 102 17/32 139 days	£ 6,648 £ 198	£ 6,372	8.00%	£ 519	7.80	Apr Oct
TREASURY 8 1/2% LN 2007	£ 9,840.06	£ 109 5/16 37 days	£ 10,756 £ 85	£ 10,000	8.50%	£ 836	7.78	Jan Jul
FIXED INTEREST TOTAL			**£ 47,247**	**£ 43,606**		**£ 3,787**	**8.16**	
EQUITY								
UNITED KINGDOM								
MINERAL EXTRACTION								
EXTRACTIVE INDUSTRIES								
RIO TINTO ORD 10P(REGD)	680	999.5p	£ 6,797	£ 6,681	£ 0.32	£ 270	3.97	Oct Apr Apr

Fig. 3. Portfolio valuation.

Laing & Cruickshank Investment Management Ltd

Portfolio Valuation

Member of The London Stock Exchange
Regulated by The Securities & Futures Authority
Member of the Credit Lyonnais Group

Date   22 Aug 1997
Ref.
Page   4

Security description	Holding	Market price	Market value	Book cost	Dividend rate	Estimated Gross income	%Div. yield	Dividends Due
BANKS, RETAIL (CONT.)								
ROYAL BANK OF SCOTLAND GROUP ORD 25P	840	593p	£ 4,981	£ 4,136	£ 0.19 II	£ 204	4.09	Jul Feb
Sector Total			£ 9,944	£ 6,781		£ 326	3.28	
INSURANCE								
COMMERCIAL UNION ORD 25P	1,320	722.5p XD	£ 9,537	£ 3,085	£ 0.31 II	£ 513	5.38	Nov May
Class Total			£ 19,481	£ 9,866		£ 839	4.31	
INVESTMENT TRUSTS								
INVESTMENT TRUSTS								
ALLIANCE TRUST ORD STK 25P	1,040	£ 24.29	£ 25,262	£ 8,652	£ 0.57 II	£ 741	2.93	Oct Apr
SECURITIES TRUST OF SCOTLAND ORD 25P	17,200	114p	£ 19,608	£ 18,463	£ 0.04	£ 806	4.11	Dec Jul
Class Total			£ 44,870	£ 27,115		£ 1,547	3.45	
EQUITY TOTAL			£ 181,235	£ 89,596		£ 7,218	3.98	
GRAND TOTAL			£ 228,482	£ 133,201		£ 11,005	4.83	

Fig. 3. Cont/d.

Laing & Cruickshank Investment Management Ltd

Portfolio Summary

Description	Book cost	Market value	Estimated Gross income	% Book cost	% Market value	% Gross income	Gross yield %
FIXED INTEREST							
FIXED INTEREST/CONVERTIBLES							
BRITISH FUNDS	£ 43,606	£ 47,247	£ 3,787	32.74	20.68	34.41	8.16
FIXED INTEREST TOTAL	£ 43,606	£ 47,247	£ 3,787	32.74	20.68	34.41	8.16
EQUITY							
MINERAL EXTRACTION							
EXTRACTIVE INDUSTRIES	£ 6,681	£ 6,797	£ 270	5.02	2.97	2.45	3.97
OIL INTEGRATED	£ 7,000	£ 11,955	£ 332	5.25	5.23	3.02	2.78
MINERAL EXTRACTION TOTAL	£ 13,681	£ 18,752	£ 602	10.27	8.21	5.47	3.21
GENERAL MANUFACTURERS							
CHEMICALS	£ 6,519	£ 9,737	£ 386	4.89	4.26	3.51	3.97
DIVERSIFIED INDUSTRIALS	£ 6,865	£ 5,043	£ 353	5.15	2.21	3.20	6.99
ENGINEERING	£ 9,559	£ 20,338	£ 950	7.18	8.90	8.64	4.67
ENGINEERING, VEHICLES	£ 5,033	£ 14,214	£ 411	3.78	6.22	3.73	2.89
GENERAL MANUFACTURERS TOTAL	£ 27,976	£ 49,333	£ 2,100	21.00	21.59	19.09	4.26
CONSUMER GOODS							
FOOD MANUFACTURERS	£ 1,496	£ 9,384	£ 348	1.12	4.11	3.17	3.71
PHARMACEUTICALS	£ 1,138	£ 14,404	£ 333	0.85	6.30	3.03	2.31
TOBACCO	£ 1,044	£ 17,168	£ 1,232	0.78	7.51	11.19	7.17
CONSUMER GOODS TOTAL	£ 3,678	£ 40,956	£ 1,913	2.76	17.93	17.38	4.67
SERVICES							
TRANSPORT							
FINANCIALS	£ 7,279	£ 7,844	£ 216	5.46	3.43	1.96	2.75
BANKS, RETAIL	£ 6,781	£ 9,944	£ 326	5.09	4.35	2.96	3.28
INSURANCE	£ 3,085	£ 9,537	£ 513	2.32	4.17	4.66	5.38
FINANCIALS TOTAL	£ 9,866	£ 19,481	£ 839	7.41	8.53	7.63	4.31
INVESTMENT TRUSTS							
INVESTMENT TRUSTS	£ 27,115	£ 44,870	£ 1,547	20.36	19.64	14.06	3.45

Fig. 3. Cont/d.

Member of The London Stock Exchange
Regulated by The Securities & Futures Authority
Member of the Credit Lyonnais Group

Laing & Cruickshank Investment Management Ltd

Portfolio Summary

Date 22 Aug 1997

Ref.

Page 6

Description	Book cost	Market value	Estimated Gross income	% Book cost	% Market value	% Gross income	Gross yield %
INVESTMENT TRUSTS (CONT.)							
EQUITY TOTAL	£ 89,596	£ 181,235	£ 7,218	67.26	79.32	65.59	3.98
GRAND TOTAL	£ 133,201	£ 226,482	£ 11,005	100.00	100.00	100.00	4.83

Fig. 3. Cont/d.

Laing & Cruickshank Investment Management Ltd

Member of the London Stock Exchange
Regulated by the Securities & Futures Authority
Member of the Credit Lyonnais Group

Portfolio Summary

Date 22 Aug 1997

Ref.

Page 7

Description	Book cost	Market value	Estimated Gross income	% Book cost	% Market value	% Gross income	Gross yield %
GEOGRAPHICAL ANALYSIS							
FIXED INTEREST							
UNITED KINGDOM	£ 43,606	£ 47,247	£ 3,787	32.74	20.68	34.41	8.16
EQUITY							
UNITED KINGDOM	£ 89,596	£ 181,235	£ 7,218	67.26	79.32	65.59	3.98
GRAND TOTAL	£ 133,201	£ 228,482	£ 11,005	100.00	100.00	100.00	4.83

Fig. 3. Cont/d.

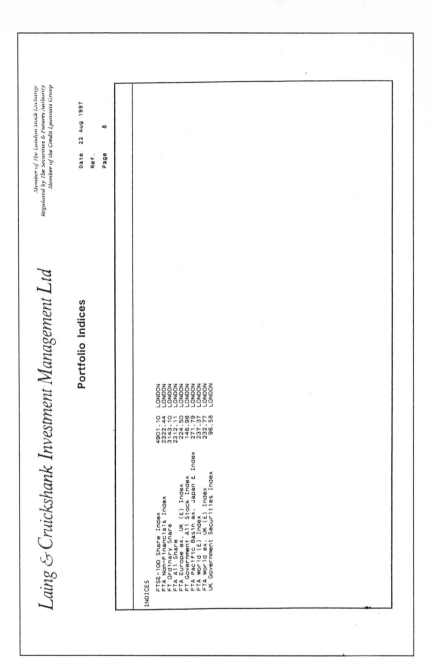

Member of The London Stock Exchange
Regulated by The Securities & Futures Authority
Member of the Credit Lyonnais Group

Laing & Cruickshank Investment Management Ltd

Portfolio Indices

INDICES

FTSE-100 Share Index	4901.10	LONDON
FTA Non-Financials Index	2322.44	LONDON
FT Ordinary Share	3143.10	LONDON
FTA All-Share	2311.10	LONDON
FTA Europe ex. UK (£) Index	224.50	LONDON
FT Government All Stock Index	146.98	LONDON
FTA Pacific Basin ex. Japan £ Index	271.79	LONDON
FTA World (£) Index	237.37	LONDON
FTA World ex. UK (£) Index	232.77	LONDON
UK Government Securities Index	96.58	LONDON

Fig. 3. Cont/d.

If you are on an advisory basis, the stockbroker would offer any advice on possible changes at the time of these valuations, or at any time in between.

If you are on a discretionary basis, the stockbroker will carry out transactions on his or her own initiative, and report to you. The effects of these changes will be shown on the periodical valuation.

If you are on an execution only basis, the stockbroker will only carry out transactions when asked by you.

Being wary

Some people are wary of giving a stockbroker control of their investments. They may be aware of the security aspect. If a stockbroker holds your portfolio on a discretionary basis, it will be held in a nominee company. There are strict rules governing these nominee companies, and the stockbrokers will have to pay a considerable amount of money as a security bond. This guarantees the investments of the investors.

The other concern some people feel is that stockbrokers may carry out transactions unnecessarily. These transactions, they fear, would not enhance their portfolio, but only generate extra commission for the stockbroker.

This practice is called 'churning'. The allusion is easy to see. The client's portfolio is like milk, being churned to produce butter for the stockbroker. However, this practice is extremely rare, especially amongst reputable brokers. If you suspect a broker of this, you can report it to the regulatory body. If found guilty, the stockbroker faces suspension.

UNDERSTANDING THE INDEX

When we talk of 'The Index', we are talking of one of the indices published by the *Financial Times*. The most commonly quoted is the FTSE 100 share index. This is an index of the prices of the 100 biggest companies quoted on the London Stock Exchange. The increase in the index gives a measure of how share prices have moved.

There are, however, several other important indices, all published by the *Financial Times*. They include The All Share index, the Ordinary Share index, the Non-Financials index, the UK Government Securities index, and the FT World index. These measure the price movements of shares in the different sectors.

The movements of these indices are often shown on graphs, with the familiar peaks and troughs. They provide a basis for comparison with the performance of other prices. For example, the price of any one share could be plotted on a graph, and then compared with the FTSE 100 index. This shows whether that share has performed better or worse than the average of the top 100. This comparison is often resorted to in considering the performance of unit trusts or investment trusts.

The indices are also sometimes used to show a correlation between share prices and other indicators, such as interest rates.

READING THE PRICES

Prices of shares are quoted each day in newspapers. The most complete list of prices is in the *Financial Times*. Other broadsheets also quote prices of most shares, and some tabloids also give prices of some of the most commonly traded shares. Figure 4 shows part of a typical day's price list.

WATER

	Price	+ or -	52 week High	Low	Market Capitalisation £ million	Yield Gross	P/E
Anglian	709	+13	727	523	1911	6.1	9.5
Severn Trent	935	-12	1085	663	1250	5.0	10.3

CHEMICALS

	Price	+ or -	52 week High	Low	Market Capitalisation £ million	Yield Gross	P/E
BOC	951	+1	1195	850	4750	3.5	16.4
Croda	445	+5	445	246	565	2.6	18.7

Fig. 4. Typical daily price listing.

The following information can be gleaned from the listings:

- Price. This is the middle price at the close of trading, and given in pence.

- + or -. This shows how the price has moved since the end of the previous day's trading.

- 52 week high/low. This shows the maximum and minimum prices that the shares have reached in the previous year.

- Market capitalisation £m. This shows the value, in millions of pounds, of the total shares in issue, multiplied by the price. This gives an idea of how big the company is.

- Yield gross. This is the actual return you would receive on your money if you invested in the shares on the day of the report.

- P/E. This is the Price/Earnings ratio. It is a key indicator in deciding about investment in a company. The price of the share is expressed in relation to the earnings per share. The earnings per share is basically the profit of the company as a whole divided by the number of shares in issue.

KNOWING THE WRINKLES

Knowing how the stock market works is one thing. What you really need to know, however, is which companies to invest in.

Blue chips

This term relates to the top companies in the country. They are usually the ones in the FTSE 100 index. They represent the companies with the soundest track record, and the strongest financial base. All companies are engaged in a business of some kind, and these are the companies which have soundly based businesses. This is not to say that things could never go wrong. There have been many spectacular failures of blue chip companies in the past.

Choosing an investment

So what factors do you look for in choosing an investment in shares?

Market sectors

You will see that the share prices quoted are divided into different sectors. These represent the types of businesses. Therefore, if you want to invest in a certain part of the economy, say, banking or leisure, because you think that will do well, you can see which quoted companies are in that sector.

It is also often more relevant to compare shares in one sector with others in that sector, rather than with other shares in different sectors, or the market as a whole.

Price-earnings ratio

This is the relationship between the price of the share and the earnings of the company (*ie* its profit). For these purposes the earnings of the company as a whole are divided by the number of shares in issue to give the earnings per share.

Example

A company has profits of £3 million. It has 10 million shares in issue. Its earnings per share are 30p.

If the price quoted for that share is £3, then the price-earnings ratio is ten. This means that the price of the share represents ten years' profit. You would then compare this ratio with the market as a whole, or with the sector in which the company operates.

Quality of earnings

If the price-earnings ratio is based on historic figures, the information is not so relevant as future earnings. Of course, the problem is that future earnings are not a known figure, whereas historic earnings are known.

The price-earnings ratio, in fact, is governed largely by 'market sentiment'. This means what the analysts employed by stockbrokers think of the company. If they have doubts about the future prospects of the company and, in particular, its ability to maintain the profit levels, then the quality of earnings is said to be low.

Dividend yield

This is also a key indicator. It represents the actual rate of return you would get if you invested in the company at the price quoted. The rate of dividend per share is based on an amount per share. The actual rate you would receive depends on the price of the share.

Example

A company declares a dividend of 5 pence per share, as the only dividend for the year. The nominal value of the share in 25 pence, so the rate of return would appear to be 20%. However, that is not relevant for these purposes. If the price of the share were £1, then the dividend yield would be 5%, because you would receive 5 pence income for every £1 you invested.

Earnings growth

This is a measure of how the company's performance has improved or otherwise. If the earnings per share of a company have shown a steady growth, then the company has obviously improved its performance year on year. If there is a dip for one year in an otherwise steady increase, then there may well be a good reason. If the earnings per share show a steady decline, you would want to find out why before investing in it.

OTHER MARKETS

The London Stock Exchange is the principal market for dealing in company shares in the UK. To qualify for inclusion, a company must satisfy certain strict requirements. However, there are other regional markets, and other markets in London. Below the level of the London Stock Exchange are the Alternative Investment Market and the Unlisted Securities Market (the AIM and the USM respectively).

These deal in a smaller number of companies' shares, and the quantity of deals in the shares are much less than the London Stock Exchange. If you have an investment in a company on the AIM or the USM, therefore, it may not be as easy to sell the shares, simply because there may not be enough, if any, buyers.

CHECKLIST

- Dealing in stocks and shares requires a stockbroker. Find one and build up a relationship with him or her.

- Decide whether to have an advisory, execution only, or discretionary service.

- Get to know the jargon, keep an eye on the prices and the index.

- Be aware of the other markets.

CASE STUDY

Charles takes the plunge on the stock market

Charles would like to invest some of his money directly into shares on the stock market. He finds a stockbroker through a work colleague and goes to see him. He listens to the advice, and makes an investment in a selection of shares recommended by the stockbroker, on an advisory basis. At first, he anxiously scans the prices almost every day, and worries when they dip. He later learns not to worry about smaller day to day fluctuations, but he still like to keep abreast of things, and takes a newspaper with a regular financial section and City report.

POINTS TO CONSIDER

1. At what point would you decide to invest directly into the stock market?

2. How would you choose a stockbroker?

3. How would you decide what service to have?

6

Choosing a Collective Investment

The seventh Commandment of Saving and Investing:

> Do not put all your eggs in one basket.

SPREADING THE RISK

Collective investments work on the principle of reducing risk by allowing you to invest in many different companies. You may not be able to have a wide variety of shares or other investments if you have a limited capital.

Collective investments work on the principle of a large number of people investing a relatively small amount, into one 'pot' (which we shall call **the fund**) and then using that fund to invest in a larger range of investments than each individual could do alone. The risk is spread, and the fund managers are able to manage the fund actively, to achieve the best results.

There are several forms of collective investment. The most common are:

● unit trusts

● investment trusts

● OEICs

● investment clubs.

Unit trusts

These are funds which accept money from new investors, and create new units in the total fund when new money is invested. When units are cashed in, those units are cancelled from the fund. The fund is set up as a trust, and trustees have oversight of the fund. Managers do the actual management of the fund. There are over 150 authorised unit trust groups in the UK and most of them manage many different funds. So there are thousands of funds to choose from.

The individual funds are usually targeted at particular sectors. For example, you may have growth funds, income funds, high income funds, extra high income funds, American funds, blue chip funds, emerging market funds, Pacific funds, and so on. The list is not quite endless, but almost.

Legally, a unit trust is governed by a trust deed. This creates a trust between the trustees (*ie* the people who are entrusted to safeguard the money) and the managers. Strictly speaking, the fund is not owned by the investors, but by the trustees for the benefit of the investors.

How it works

When a unit trust receives new money from an investor, it creates new units in the fund. When an investor wishes to cash in his investment, the unit trust pays out the money and cancels the units. This is the main difference between units trusts and investment trusts.

This feature means that it is an 'open-end fund'.

The price of units in each fund is quoted daily in the financial press and in the financial pages of daily newspapers. The prices, updated daily, are arrived at by totalling the values of all the shares owned by the fund, and dividing that between the number of units in issue. This is another difference between unit trusts and investment trusts.

Question

What if I have shares, and want to invest instead in unit trusts?

Answer

Many unit trusts will accept shares in lieu of payment, provided that the shares are already on their investment list. The shares are taken in by the unit trust at their market value, with no deduction for dealing expenses, and an equivalent value of the units is credited to you. This can be an economic way of getting into unit trusts from shares.

Investment trusts

These are limited liability companies, and are quoted on the Stock Exchange. They have a limited capital, and if you wish to buy shares in an investment trust company, you have to buy them on the Stock Exchange. This means, in effect, that you are buying the shares from somebody else. This feature means that it is a 'closed-end fund'. It also means that you as a shareholder are the legal owner of a proportion of the company's assets.

The investment company itself invests in other companies, in much the same way that unit trusts do. Usually, however, the investment trust company does not act as an 'umbrella' with several funds. Each investment trust company has its own investment strategy, and invests within its plan.

As we have seen, investment trusts are quoted companies on the Stock Exchange. The price of the shares is determined in the same way as prices of other shares – that is, by supply and demand. Thus, the total value of their shares can be arrived at by multiplying the price by the total number of shares in issue. This is known as the market capitalisation.

By comparing this with the market value of all shares which the company owns (its investments), you can arrive at a generally used indicator for investment trusts. It is usual in present conditions to find that the shares of investment trust companies stand at a discount to the value of the shares it holds as investments. The amount of this discount is an indicator of market sentiment towards the Investment Trust.

OEICs

This abbreviation stands for 'Open Ended Investment Companies'. As its name suggests, it combines the open-ended nature of units trusts with the company legal structure of investment trusts.

A particular feature of OEICs is that prices are given as one price for buyers or sellers. This contrasts with both unit trusts and investment trusts, where there is a price spread between the price to a buyer and the price to a seller.

Investment clubs

As the name suggests, this is a more informal type of collective investment. It consists of a number of people getting together (usually on a regular basis) to make their investment plans. Obviously, as the number of people involved is much smaller, there is not so much money to invest, and the members are usually amateurs. However, it does give the members more direct say in the investment of their money. Also, it provides a social occasion.

Because money is involved, it is necessary to have rules and a proper control system to safeguard the money and investments.

The development of the Internet has also seen the emergence of 'investment clubs' on the net. These are more informal, because the club members only exchange information, and tips, rather than pooling their money.

CHOOSING A COLLECTIVE INVESTMENT

You are now ready to make an investment in a collective fund. What is available to you, and how should you decide? Many sectors of funds are available, but basically, they fall within the following main categories.

- growth funds
- income funds
- high income funds
- geographical funds
- ethical funds
- split capital funds
- small companies funds
- tracker funds
- fund of funds
- gilt and fixed interest funds
- tax protected funds
- corporate bond funds.

What do they mean?

What is the investment bias or aim of each type of fund? Most of them are fairly obvious from their titles, but here is a brief summary.

Growth funds
These are slanted towards capital growth rather than income. They therefore provide a lower income than you might otherwise expect, and can be considered a slightly higher risk profile than income funds.

Income funds
These are geared to produce an income which has a realistic possibility of growing each year to at least keep pace with inflation. The income would normally be expanded to approximate to the yield on the shares making up the FTSE 100 index. In practice, many fund managers actually do better than this, and the income is often higher than the FTSE 100 yield. In theory, the capital growth potential should not be so good on these funds, but in practice, historically they have proved to have a good capital growth record.

High income funds
These are geared to produce a higher than average income, but this will not have as realistic a chance of increasing each year in line with inflation as pure income funds. The additional income is generated by mixing with ordinary shares, various fixed interest investments in the form of Government stocks, preference shares, debentures, *etc.* Obviously, the opportunities for capital growth are much more restricted.

Geographical funds
As the name implies, these funds invest in a particular area of the globe. Typical funds might be 'Far East', 'American', 'Pacific', 'European', 'Eastern European' or 'Emerging Markets'. These funds should be considered as a higher risk, and you should approach them with only as much confidence as you have in the economies of those geographical areas. If you do not know enough, or are not willing to trust an adviser implicitly, you would be better advised to stay away from these funds. Otherwise, any news broadcast could cause you great anxiety, as you see what is happening all over the world.

Ethical funds
We will look at these in some more depth in a later chapter. Suffice it to say that they are funds which either avoid certain negative factors, or which actively invest in certain positive factors. These are funds for true believers.

Split capital funds
These are funds in which the units or shares are in two classes — income or capital. One class gets all the capital growth, the other class gets all the income. This obviously gives a higher capital growth to capital shares or units, and higher income to income shares or units than would otherwise be the case.

Small companies funds
These may also sometimes be called 'Opportunity Funds'. They invest in smaller companies which the managers believe have good growth opportunities. Again, it is self-evident that they are a higher risk investment, but carry the opportunity for higher capital growth.

Tracker funds
These are funds that 'track' the movement of various stock market indices. They do this by investing in the same companies as the companies whose shares are included in the index concerned. Thus, there are

funds for example tracking the FTSE 100 index, the FTSE All Share index, the Dow Jones index, the Nikkei index, the Hang Seng index, and so on.

These type of funds therefore do not rely on active trading by the managers, since the investments are relatively stable and unchanging, Investments are only bought or sold when there is any change to the investments included on an index. In the recent past, for instance, when some of the larger building societies demutualised and became companies, they were included on the FTSE 100 index, and tracker fund managers had to adjust their holdings.

Otherwise, there is so little active management that the annual management fee on these funds is usually considerably lower than other types of funds. Many people invest in them for this reason, and because they have little faith in investment managers 'beating' the major indices.

Fund of funds
These funds invest in other unit trusts or investment trusts. This spreads the investment risk even further, and can be considered a lower risk investment. However, because of the wide spread of investments, the income performance is not usually spectacularly good.

Gilt and fixed interest funds
These funds, as the name indicates, are invested in government securities and other fixed interest stock. They provide a spread of risk for those who wish to obtain the best fixed interest returns available.

Tax protected funds
These include Personal Equity Plans (PEPs), which provided a tax free environment for income and capital gains. A maximum of £6,000 per person could be invested in these, but they were replaced by Individual Savings Accounts (ISAs) in April 1999 and existing PEPs may be transferred to them.

Corporate bond funds
These funds are invested in company fixed interest borrowings, such as bonds and debentures. They are most common in PEP and ISA products. They offer investors a high return tax free income (when in a PEP or ISA) but very limited capital growth.

CHECKLIST

- Spread the risk by using collective investments.

- Use a unit trust, an investment trust, an OEIC, or join an investment club.

- Choose the type of trust you want, and invest in one or a selection of trusts.

CASE STUDY

Derek chooses unit trusts

Derek is a new 'case study'. He is in his forties, and has inherited a sum from a relative, just over £25,000. He decides he would not like to invest directly in the Stock Exchange, mainly because it has a 'mystique' which he does not understand. However, he would like to invest in British industry and business. He decides that he would like to use unit trusts. They have a more 'approachable' image. He invests in growth funds, to build up his capital, with a view to transferring to income funds when he retires.

He puts £5,000 in an ISA and then £5,000 into each of three other growth funds, with different unit trusts. This makes a total of £20,000 invested. He keeps the remaining £5,000 in a 'rainy day' account. He plans to transfer a further £5,000 each year into an ISA as long as they are available.

POINTS TO CONSIDER

1. What proportion (if any) of your capital do you think you should invest in collective investments?

2. How would you feel about having to cash in other investments to put money in collective investments?

7

Investing in Your Country

'As safe as the Bank of England' is a phrase that denotes absolute security. Certainly there is a place in everybody's savings or investment plans for secure investments backed by the government. These days, there is quite a wide choice, so most people should be able to find something which meets their needs.

GOVERNMENT STOCKS

In the same way that companies need to raise money by borrowing from the public, the government also do this. They do this by issuing stocks, most of which have a fixed repayment date, and a fixed rate of interest. This is a really low risk form of investment, and is used by many people for just that feature. For this reason, they are often referred to as **gilts**. Many people with a portfolio of other investments also include a proportion of money in government stocks.

They are referred to under a series of names, including the following:

- Treasury stock
- Exchequer stock
- Consols (short for Consolidated stock)
- Funding stock
- Convertible stock
- War loan.

Whatever name they bear, they are basically the same – by investing in them, you are lending the government money.

They are also quoted on the Stock Exchange, and for those purposes, they are divided into:

- short dated (up to five years)
- medium dated (five to 15 years)
- long dated (over 15 years)

● undated

● index linked.

The short, medium and long dates refer to the redemption date. Undated stocks have no redemption date, and in theory could go on for ever. There are only three of these stocks currently in issue.

The stocks are **redeemed at par** (apart from the index linked stocks). That is to say, the repayment of the amount loaned is made on the stated date, at the same nominal amount at which they were issued. This may not be the same as the amount you paid, since their value fluctuates on the stock market according to prevailing rates of interest.

Index linked stocks are ones which have a redemption date, but they are not repaid at par. The amount at which they are repaid is linked to the change in the retail prices index between the issue date and the redemption date.

Example
If an index linked stock was issued when the retail prices index stood at 100, and then repaid when the index stood at 200, the amount repaid would be twice the original nominal amount of the stock.

Because there is this inbuilt gain in the capital (in theory, the index could actually be lower at redemption, but this possibility is so remote as to be out of the reckoning), the interest rate paid on these stocks is relatively low. Of the index linked stocks in issue at present, the interest rates range between 2.5% and 4.375%.

Interest
Interest is paid twice yearly on government stocks. It is paid with income tax deducted at source. If you are not liable to tax, you may apply to the Inland Revenue to have the tax refunded.

Buying government stocks on the National Savings Register
As an alternative to buying government stocks on the Stock Exchange, you may buy them from National Savings. There is a small charge for this, but it is not usually as much as buying them on the Stock Exchange. The other main advantage of buying them this way is that the interest is paid gross – *ie* with no income tax deducted. However, the interest is taxable. This is often the preferred option for those whose income level means that they are not liable to income tax. The vast majority of government stocks are on the National Savings Register and available to buy in this way.

Prices of government stocks

Government stocks are quoted on the Stock Exchange, and the price is quoted as a figure for which you may buy or sell £100 worth of the nominal value of stock. Prices, by tradition, are given in fractions up to thirty-seconds. See Figure 5 for a daily listing.

SHORTS (under 5 years)

	52 weeks			Interest	Redemption
	Price	High	Low	+ or −	Yield	Yield
Treasury 8% 2000	103	104	102	+1	7.7	6.49
Convertible 9% 2000	104	106	103		8.6	6.5

MEDIUMS (5 to 15 years)

Treasury 9% 2008	122	124	106	+1	7.33	6.04
Convertible 9% 2011	126	127	109		7.12	6.08

Fig. 5 Government stocks daily price listing.

Thus, any particular stock can be priced over 100, in which case it is said to be at a premium, or under 100, which is said to be at a discount. The price is governed by the prevailing interest rates at the time. For example, if prevailing interest rates are around 8%, and the nominal interest rate on a stock is 12%, the demand for that stock is likely to be high, and the price will rise above 100. In fact, in this case, unless the stock had a very short life to redemption, the price would rise to about 150, so that the yield would be roughly equivalent to the prevailing rates.

Yields

The financial press, in quoting prices for government stocks, gives yield figures. This means, as we have seen, the actual return which you will get on your money, and unless the price is 100, it will be different from the nominal interest rate of the stock. However, there are two yields quoted, an interest yield and a redemption yield.

Interest yield

The interest yield is the actual yield which you would receive on your money if you invested. This is simple to see, as in the example given above. If a stock with a nominal interest rate of 12% is quoted at 150, the interest yield will be 8%.

Redemption yield

The redemption yield is an additional indicator. It can be calculated because government stocks have a fixed redemption date (Therefore it is not quoted for undated stocks.) It represents the 'real' yield you would get over the remaining life of the stock. In other words, it takes into account the premium or the discount in the price.

I have called this the 'real' yield, because it is important to bear this factor in mind when comparing prices and yields. It is shown at its most extreme in very short dated stocks. For example, in July 1997, the following price appeared in the financial press.

Exchequer 15% 1997 – price 102.5 – interest yield 14.63% – redemption yield 6.62%.

Therefore, with the price at 102.5, it might have appeared a good bargain to buy a 15% stock. However, the stock was dated 1997, and only had a few months to go before redemption – in fact, there was only one more half yearly interest payment due. This meant also that in a few months' time, the stock for which you had paid 102.5 would be redeemed at par – *ie* at 100.

In fact, as you would expect, the redemption yields of stocks with similar life spans are very similar, even though the interest yield may be quite different.

NATIONAL SAVINGS

National Savings are also a government department, and once again when you invest in National Savings, you are lending money to the government. National Savings have several different products. These are:

- National Savings Bank Ordinary Accounts

- National Savings Bank Investment Accounts

- National Savings Certificates

- Premium Bonds

- National Savings Income Bonds

- National Savings Capital Bonds

- National Savings Pensioners' Guaranteed Income Bonds

- National Savings Fixed Rate Savings Bonds

- National Savings Children's Bonus Bonds.

Each of these have different features, as follows.

National Savings Bank

This is, as the name implies, a savings bank which operates through all post offices. The only accounts available are the following two.

National Savings Bank Ordinary Accounts
This is a savings account which gives a low rate of interest (at the time of writing this was 1.25% on balances up to £500, and 1.35% on balances from £500 upwards). There is a minimum investment of £20, and a maximum of £10,000. The interest is variable, paid gross, and the first £70 per year of interest is tax free.

National Savings Bank Investment Accounts
This is a savings account which requires one month's notice for withdrawals. It gives higher rates of interest than the ordinary account (at the time of writing, variable up to 5.1%). There is a minimum investment of £20, and a maximum of £100,000. Higher rates of interest are paid on balances over £500. The interest is variable, paid gross, but is liable to tax.

National Savings Certificates

There are fixed interest certificates and index linked certificates.

Fixed Interest Certificates

These are certificates issued by the National Savings office. You buy certificates in any amount from £100 to £10,000. The interest is guaranteed for the five year term of the certificate. The interest is also free of tax. However, you may not draw on the interest before the five year term is finished. If you need to cash in the certificates before the five year term, the interest rate is lower for the earlier years. If you do not cash in the certificates at the end of the five year term, they continue to earn interest, but only at a variable rate called the "General Extension Rate". This is lower than the normal rate on certificates.

Index Linked Certificates

These certificates are also issued for five year terms, and again you may invest from £100 to £10,000. The value at the end of the five year term is calculated in two parts.

One part is the index linked part. This means that the certificate's value increases by the increase in the retail prices index over the five year period.

The other part is the interest. Interest is given at a lower rate than the fixed interest certificates, and added to the value at the end of the five year term.

If you need to cash in early, the index linking applies after the first anniversary of the purchase, and interest is also added from that date, but at a lower rate. If you do not cash in the certificates at the end of the five year term, they continue to earn index linked 'extension terms', which are lower than the current rate on new issues.

Premium Bonds
You may invest a minimum of £100 to a maximum of £20,000 in Premium Bonds. They do not pay interest, but once you have held the Bonds for a full calendar month, your number goes into the prize draw.

There is one prize of £1 million every month, and a number of other prizes from £50 to £100,000. Each £1 unit has a fixed chance of 19,000 to 1 of winning a prize every month. The size of the prize fund determines how many prizes of each denomination there are (except the 'jackpot' prize of £1 million, one of which is guaranteed every month). The prize fund is determined by a notional rate of interest on the total value of Premium Bons in issue.

The Bonds may be cashed in at any time without notice, at the same value for which they were purchased. The prizes are exempt from tax.

National Savings Income Bonds
You may invest a minimum of £500 up to a maximum of £1,000,000 in Income Bonds. They pay monthly interest at a variable rate, and the interest is paid gross – i.e. without deduction of income tax. The interest is taxable. The interest rate is fairly competitive, and a higher rate of interest applies for investments of £25,000 or more. Three months notice is required for withdrawal, although you may cash them in without notice, but with a penalty equivalent to 90 days interest.

National Savings Capital Bonds
You may invest a minimum of £100 up to a maximum of £250,000 in Capital Bonds. This is a lump sum investment with a fixed term of 5 years, and a fixed, guaranteed interest rate for the whole 5 year term. However, the interest rate is 'tiered'. This means that the interest starts at a lower figure for the first year, then increases each year to make up the full guaranteed amount at the end of the 5 year term.

The interest is not paid to you, but added to the amount of the Bond. National Savings send you a statement every year to show how the Bond has grown with the added interest. The interest is added gross, and the amount of the interest is taxable. You may cash in the Bond at any time without notice. Repayment is then made of the amount standing to your credit at the previous anniversary of the purchase, plus interest from then at the rate of interest for the last year. Thus, early cashing in means that you lose out on the full interest rate.

National Savings Pensioners' Guaranteed Income Bonds

You must be over 60 years of age to buy these Bonds. You may invest a minimum of £500, up to a maximum of £1,000,000 in these Bonds. They are five year bonds and two year bonds.

The interest is at a guaranteed fixed rate for the term. Interest is paid monthly, and is paid gross. However, it is taxable.

You may cash in these Bonds early, but at 60 days notice, and during the notice period, no interest is paid. Alternatively, you may cash them in without notice, but subject to a penalty of 90 days interest on the amount withdrawn.

National Savings Fixed Rate Savings Bonds

You may invest a minimum of £500 and a maximum of £1,000,000 in these Bonds. Interest is paid monthly or annually, at a guaranteed rate for a period, but with tax deducted at source.

These Bonds are offered with four different fixed terms, of 6 months, 1 year, 18 months, or 3 years. The rate of interest depends on the term you choose, and the rate is tiered, with different rates for investments from £500 up to £20,000, from £20,000 up to £50,000, and over £50,000.

The Bonds are held for their full term, then National Savings will tell you what your options are at the completion of the term.

National Savings Children's Bonus Bonds

These may be opened by anyone over the age of 15, for anyone under that age. The minimum investment is £25, and the maximum £1,000. These figures are for each person on whose behalf the investment is made. Thus, a parent may put in up to £1,000 for each of their children, or any other children. The bonds are controlled by the child's parent or legal guardian, irrespective of who made the actual investment of money.

Interest is at a fixed guaranteed rate for five years. At the end of the five year term, a bonus is added to the investment. This bonus is also fixed and guaranteed at the outset. The interest and the bonus are exempt from income tax.

When interest rates are changed, a new issue of these bonds is made. At that point, a new investment may be made in the new issue on top of what has already been invested.

These bonds may be cashed in early without notice, but again there is a loss of interest. Repayment will be made of the amount of the bond at the previous anniversary, plus interest at a daily rate up to the time of cashing in. Bonuses are not paid until the full five year term is finished. The bond may also be cashed in on the child's 21st birthday.

CHECKLIST

● Government stocks and National Savings products are a low risk form of investment.

● Some are dated, some are index linked.

● There is a wide range to choose from.

● Some are only available to restricted classes of people.

CASE STUDIES

Alison dabbles with Premium Bonds

Alison has always had a National Savings account and some Premium Bonds, which her parents started for her when she was a child. She keeps these open, not with any serious amounts of money, but just for the sake of keeping them open. And who knows, she may come up trumps with her Premium Bonds.

Charles opts for age-related bonds

Being of the right age, Charles decides to put some money into Pensioners' Guaranteed Income Bonds. These give a high rate of interest, and are guaranteed for five years. He decides it will give a good mix with some other equity based investments.

POINTS TO CONSIDER

1. Do you feel any differently about investing in your country to investing in a commercial enterprise?

2. Do you feel that investing in any of the index-linked investments allays your fears about inflation?

3. What proportion of your total money do you think you should put in gilts or National Savings Products? Why?

8

Planning for Your Retirement

Here is the eighth Commandment of Saving and Investing:

> You are never too young to start saving.

Your retirement is the longest holiday you are going to take. Make sure that you provide adequately to enjoy that holiday. The basic state pension does not really give an income adequate for most people's expectations. You may, of course, try to save for your retirement in any way you like. Simply putting money away in a savings account could be one way of tackling it, although it is unlikely to do the trick.

However, the tax incentives to provide for retirement are amongst the most generous there are. You have every encouragement to save for your retirement, in ways that are government approved and attract tax relief.

SERPS (State Earnings Related Pension Scheme)

If you are employed, you will be paying National Insurance Contributions. This is made up of a basic contribution and an additional earnings related contribution. The earnings related contribution goes towards providing you with an additional earnings related pension when you retire.

Contracting out

You may opt to contract out of the SERPS scheme. In that case, any additional contributions that would have gone to the SERPS scheme must be diverted to a private pension scheme. This will be operated by your employer if there is a superannuation scheme. Otherwise, you will have to arrange your own scheme.

SUPERANNUATION SCHEMES

These are schemes run by employers to provide a pension when you retire. This need not necessarily be at the age of 65. Many employers these days provide for retirement much earlier. These schemes may be contributory or non-contributory. A contributory scheme is one in which you contribute. The employer's contribution may be related to the contribution you make (*eg* the employer may match any contribution you make up to a certain percentage of your salary) or it may be unrelated to your contribution.

Provided that the superannuation scheme meets the requirements of the Inland Revenue, contributions are tax deductable.

Benefits

Under an employer's superannuation scheme, the benefits at retirement may be a **final salary scheme**, or a **money purchase scheme**. A final salary scheme is one in which the pension is set at a proportion of your final salary at the date you retire, geared to the number of years' contributions you have made. Thus, it may be expressed as, say, one sixtieth of your final salary for every complete year you have contributed to the scheme.

A money purchase scheme operates in a different way. The contributions you make are credited to a fund, and at your retirement the fund is used to purchase an annuity.

Lump sums

Both types of scheme usually provide for part of the fund or pension to be commuted in return for a tax free lump sum.

Death in service benefits

Both types of scheme also provide for a benefit to your dependants if you die before retiring. This is also based on either the salary at date of death, or the amount accumulated in the fund.

Additional voluntary contributions

As the names implies, this means that you may make additional contributions to the superannuation scheme. The total contributions may not exceed 15 per cent of your salary.

STAKEHOLDER PENSIONS

At the time of writing, Stakeholder Pensions are in the planning stage – they will be introduced early in 2001. They are aimed mainly at those earning in the range of £10,000 - £20,000 per year. They will have to be offered by employers, and they will incur only minimal charges. There will also be the opportunity for self employed or even non employed people to take out Stakeholder Pensions and still benefit from full tax relief.

PERSONAL PENSIONS

These are plans, approved by the Inland Revenue and run by large insurance and pension companies, which are long term savings schemes, designed to provide for retirement. Because of the generous tax advantages, they have rules which must be adhered to in order to qualify for the tax concessions.

Qualifying earnings

Firstly, you must have qualifying earnings to be able to put your money into one of these schemes. This means that your earnings must come from:

● self-employment, or

● employment with an employer which does not have a pension scheme of its own, or

● furnished holiday letting income.

If you do not have earnings which qualify, the Inland Revenue can instruct the pension company to repay to you the contributions you have paid.

Benefits

The other main condition is that the benefits can only be paid to you within a certain age range. For personal pension plans, this age range is between 50 and 75. There are, however, several categories of occupation which allow earlier retirement for the purposes of drawing benefits. These include many sports activities, such as wrestlers, downhill skiers, footballers, jockeys, *etc*, as well as other types of occupation, such as models and dancers.

The pension you receive is an annuity purchased by your fund. An annuity is a regular sum, paid monthly, quarterly or annually, for the rest of your life. The rates are worked out by actuaries.

Annuities can be of fixed amounts or escalating amounts. The increases can be of a fixed amount each year (such as five per cent), or linked to the retail prices index. The annuities can also be for the sole life of the beneficiary, or for the joint lives of the beneficiary and his or her spouse. A minimum guarantee period of, say, five years can be provided if requested. This means that if the beneficiary dies within that period, the survivors get the income for the rest of that guarantee period. There are also 'impaired life' annuities. This means that if the beneficiary is suffering from a life threatening illness, then because the life expectancy is not so long, the annuity rate is increased.

Death benefit

If you die before taking the retirement benefits, then the pension policy will state what benefit your dependants will receive. In some older retirement annuity policies, the death benefit was only a return of contributions, or return of contributions plus a nominal rate of interest. Currently, the best practice is for the value of the accumulated fund to be paid as the death benefit. This is certainly one of the key points to look for in a policy.

Tax free lump sum

When you take your pension, you need not take all of it in the form of a regular pension. Part of the fund may be taken as a tax free lump sum. At present, the regulations allow you to take up to 25 per cent of the fund as a lump sum. It is nearly always beneficial to take this lump sum. This allows you to invest the lump sum, enjoy the income, and still have the capital available if you need it, or to pass on to your survivors. Clearly this is better because otherwise the whole fund is tied up in the annuity, and there is no access to the capital.

Open market option

When the policy matures, and you want to take your pension, you have the right to take the fund from your pension company, and 'shop around' for the best value annuity. This is because the pension offered by each company is determined by its own annuity rates. These rates vary, and shopping around enables you to find the best value. This 'open market option' must be written into the pension contract to enable it to qualify for the tax advantages.

Pensions mis-selling

Some years ago, there was much publicity about some pension companies whose sales forces had sold the wrong sort of personal pension policies to people. The reason for this was that the salespeople got a lot of commission. The people who bought these policies were wrongly advised, and would probably have done better to stay in their employer's schemes. At the time of writing, the pension companies are in the process of compensating the customers.

CHOOSING A POLICY

If you are considering taking out a policy, there are a bewildering number of choices available, and an equally bewildering number of salespeople trying to sell them to you. Bear in mind that they are earning their living, in the form of commission on these policies. The adviser you use may be independent or an employee of the company, but they still have a living to earn. Some companies advertise the fact that they do not pay commission to intermediaries. However, they still have their own sales force to pay.

However, the fact that a salesperson gets commission does not necessarily mean that what they are trying to sell you is not good value. The following are some points to look for when choosing a pension.

What is the basis of the fund growth?

The funds are usually **unit linked** or **with profit**. Unit linked means that the premiums buy you a certain number of units in a fund or funds provided by the pension company. Like unit trusts, there are various types of funds. The prices are quoted in the financial press, and the value of your pension fund at any time is the value of the units, multiplied by the number of units you hold. This means, of course, that the value can fall as well as rise.

With profit funds means that the investment profits each year are credited to your account, as a 'bonus declaration'. The bonuses are added to the value of your fund each year, and there is also usually a 'terminal bonus' added when the policy matures. The annual bonuses cannot be taken away once they have been added for your fund. Although it may seem preferable to have profits added in this way, the 'with profit' policies usually keep a reserve back in good years to even out the growth.

What is the charging structure?

Many companies pay commission, and, particularly in the case of 'regular premium' policies, this means there is a large deduction from your fund in the first year or two. Thus, it could take your fund a few years to recuperate from this reduction. This is known as 'front end loading'.

How flexible is the policy?

Do you want to pay regular premiums, or a single premium? Does your policy give you the opportunity to suspend premiums if necessary? If you are paying regular monthly or yearly premiums, can you add on single premiums at a later date?

What is the basis of the benefit if you should die before taking the pension?

You should always look for the fund value as the benefit, rather than return of premiums, even with interest.

Retirement annuity policies

These were the precursor to the personal pension schemes. They were available to self employed people in the traditional 'with profit' format, or 'unit linked'. Although these are no longer available to start as new policies, many people who started these policies still have them in force. They were similar in many ways to the personal pension policies, but the rules differed in some respects. One of the main differences is that the age at which benefits may be taken is between 60 and 75. Also, the tax free lump sum is calculated differently from the personal pension policies, and is usually rather more.

INCOME DRAWDOWNS

Since 1995 it has been possible to opt for an income drawdown instead of taking the full benefits at retirement age. The theory is that annuity rates may not be particularly advantageous when you want to start drawing your pension. This has meant in the past that you could have been 'locked in' to a mediocre annuity rate for the rest of your life. The opportunity is now there for you to defer taking the full benefits from your pension fund, but instead to 'draw down' a certain amount each year from the fund – within certain limits, of course. The fund continues, but is depleted by the drawdowns each year, until such time as the benefits are taken, which must be done by the age of 75.

Most companies only allow drawdown schemes for pension funds of £100,000 or more. A possible disadvantage is the fact that insurance companies are offering higher than usual commission to intermediaries for drawdown schemes than for the normal annuities. This has led to the fear that drawdowns could be recommended even when they may not be the best value.

PHASED RETIREMENT

If the amount in your pension fund is adequate, you could opt for phased retirement. This is particularly useful for a person who wishes to retire from work gradually. If you have been able to make contributions to several different funds, you could start taking benefits from one of the funds, while reducing the amount you work, and gradually take benefits from the other funds year by year, until you reach full retirement.

If you have not been able to contribute to several funds, some companies will allow you to convert your pension fund into a number of smaller funds, and to phase the benefits from them. As with income drawdown, however, this sort of scheme will normally only be considered for funds in excess of £100,000.

CHECKLIST

- Approved pension plans and superannuation schemes are amongst the best long term savings opportunities. They give tax relief at the highest rate, and provide attractive alternatives when taking the benefits. However, the capital is locked up absolutely until the benefits can be taken.

- Superannuation schemes, available if you are employed, may be contributory or non-contributory. They may be based on money purchase benefits, or final salary benefits. There is also the government SERPS, which, however, you may contract out of.

- Personal pension policies are available if you are in non-pensionable employment or in self-employment. Retirement annuity policies are no longer available but many are still in force. Policies may be with profit or unit linked. They may also be linked with mortgages.

- Drawdown schemes are available – but usually only for funds in excess of £100,000. Phased retirement can also be planned into the benefits.

CASE STUDIES

Alison joins her firm's superannuation scheme

Alison secures a job, and finds that it qualifies for joining the firm's superannuation scheme, under which her contributions are matched by the company. She decides on a modest amount to start saving, confident that she can take it with her if she should change jobs in the future.

Brian increases his contributions

Brian has been saving with his company's superannuation scheme for some years. He now feels that he can put more savings in, and in fact this is a main concern of his. He looks around, and asks his company about the opportunities for putting more into their scheme. He decides to put as much as he can into the company scheme, and if there is any left over, to put it into a personal pension policy.

POINTS TO CONSIDER

1. Do you feel that you can put off providing for your retirement until later? If so, have you done the sums?

2. Have you considered all the options open to you?

3. Do you feel that you need to take advice about your pensions?

9

Benefiting from Incentives

Here is the ninth Commandment of Saving and Investing:

> Never let the incentive tail wag the investment dog.

Incentives exist on several forms of investments, and the incentive which most readily springs to mind is tax exemption in some form or other.

Incentives should never be the sole reason for making a certain type of investment. However, incentives can make certain types of investment more attractive than a similar investment without the incentive.

TAX BREAKS

Some types of investments and savings benefit from tax incentives. This is because the government wants to promote savings in general, or the particular type of investment involved. Here are some of the types of savings and investments which attract tax incentives.

National Savings Bank Ordinary Account
The first £70 of interest each year on these accounts is exempt from income tax.

National Savings Certificates
The interest and index linking increases on National Savings Certificates (both fixed interest and index linked) are exempt from income tax and capital gains tax.

Government securities
Most government securities are exempt from capital gains tax on any profit made on selling them.

Personal Equity Plans (PEPs)

PEPs were replaced by ISAs in April 1999. However, any investments made in PEPs before that date retain their tax free status. You can also switch PEPs from their existing funds into any new PEP fund you wish.

Tax Exempt Special Savings Accounts

TESSAs were replaced by ISAs in April 1999. They were 5 year savings plans, and any TESSA started before April 1999 will continue until it matures. Any TESSAs reaching the end of their 5 year life may be cashed in, or the original capital (but not the interest accrued) may be transferred to a TESSA ISA.

Individual savings accounts (ISAs)

This is the new form of tax free savings introduced in April 1999.

- You may invest up to £7,000 a year until 5th April 2001. Thereafter the limit is due to be reduced to £5,000. Within this limit, up to £3,000 (£1,000 after 5th April 2001) may be put in a cash ISA, and up to £1,000 in a life assurance.

- An ISA may include any combination of cash, insurance, or shares (including unit trusts and OEICs).

- Up to three 'mini' ISAs may be opened each year, for each of the three elements.

- A 'maxi' ISA including all three elements may only be managed by one manager for each year.

- You can transfer existing TESSAs or PEPs into an ISA.

Pensions

The government encourages people to provide for their retirement by giving tax incentives to the premiums paid. At present, these attract full tax relief at the top marginal rate of income tax to which the person paying the premium is liable. Until recently, the pension fund itself also benefited from tax relief on the income it generated.

When the pension becomes payable, some of the pension fund may be commuted to a tax free lump sum instead of being paid as a pension. The present limit for this is 25 per cent of the fund, for personal pension plans. For further details, see Chapter 8.

Capital gains tax re-investment relief

If an asset has been sold producing a gain chargeable to capital gains tax, the gain may be deferred by re-investing the proceeds of sale (or sometimes a smaller amount) into ordinary shares in unquoted companies. A company is unquoted if it is not quoted on a recognised Stock Exchange or on the Unlisted Securities Market. However, it can be quoted on the Alternative Investment Market.

Some investment houses specialise in recommending these companies which qualify for the re-investment relief.

Friendly Societies

Friendly Societies are allowed to issue 'tax exempt life or endowment policies'. There is, however, a limit of £25 per month (or £270 yearly) on the premiums payable. However, within this modest amount, all the gains are free of any tax.

Employee share schemes

These are schemes designed to encourage employee loyalty. The schemes reward employees when, as a result of their work, the company performs well. They allow employees to save regularly and buy shares in the company at a discounted rate. The gains on the shares are free from tax. There are three basic types of scheme.

SAYE (Save as you earn)
Under this scheme, employees save between £5 and £250 per month, for a fixed term of either three, five or seven years. At the end of that term, there is a tax free bonus. For a three year term, the bonus is three times the monthly premium; for a five year term, nine times the monthly premium; and for a seven year term, the bonus is 18 times the monthly premium. The money in the SAYE account at the end of the term can be taken out in cash, or in the form of shares bought at an option price of up to 20 per cent discount on the market value at the outset of the contract term. This scheme must be open to all employees.

Profit share scheme
Under this scheme, employees are given free shares which are held in trust for them. The maximum value of shares given to any employee is the greater of

● £3,000 or

● 10 per cent of annual salary (up to a maximum of £8,000).

The shares must stay in the trust for at least two years in any case, and for at least three years if the employee wants the shares free of income tax. However, the employee may have to pay capital gains tax on the difference between the sale price and the market value of the shares when they were issued. Some of the schemes operate on the basis of employees having to buy a number of shares, and the company matches that number with free shares. It is a 'buy one, get one free' scheme. This scheme must also be open to all employees of a company.

Company share option scheme
This type of scheme does not have to be open to all employees, and is sometimes known as 'executive share option scheme'. This is the type of scheme which has earned some directors the title 'fat cats'. They have made more on these share options than their salary. The company grants the employee concerned the option to buy company shares at a determined price. To benefit from tax relief, the option must be exercised between three years and ten years from the date the option is granted.

Aesops
Under an all employee share option plan announced in the March 2000 budget, companies will be able to give employees up to £3,000 of shares a year, free of tax and National Insurance. Employees will be able to buy shares in a 'partnership' scheme, and the employer can also award shares to employees for reaching performance targets. The maximum allowed for purchases and awards together is £1,500 per year. The employer can then match any shares up to a two for one basis, thereby allowing them to give £3,000 of shares per year. All of this will be free of tax and National Insurance.

Capital Gains Tax on shareholdings
Under measures announced in the March 2000 budget, certain shareholdings will benefit from the accelerated tapering relief. This means that if you have owned the shares for four years, Capital Gains Tax will be charged at a maximum of 10%.

This applies to the following types of shares –

● All shareholdings in unquoted companies

● All shareholdings held by employees in quoted companies

● Shareholdings of more than 5% of the total capital in quoted companies

The above categories of shares qualify as 'business assets' for the purposes of the accelerated tapering relief.

Venture Capital Trusts and Enterprise Investment Scheme

Under these government approved schemes, you get a 20% income tax relief on investments in these schemes. The shares must be held for a minimum period (which was reduced in the March 2000 budget from five years to three years), or the relief given will be clawed back.

Venture Capital Trusts also qualify as 'unquoted' shares for the purposes of capital gains tax re-investment relief (see above).

OTHER INCENTIVES

Shareholder concessions

Some companies offer shareholders concessions, usually in the form of discounts on the company's products or services. Some of these require a minimum shareholding, and some offers are for limited periods.

If you use one company's services or products often, you may find the concessions useful. For example, if you travel frequently to the continent, you may find it useful to take advantage of Eurotunnel's or P and O's discounts to shareholders on fares.

Otherwise, do not let these incentives over-ride a decision taken on otherwise purely investment criteria.

CHECKLIST

Tax incentives exist (or will exist) on various forms of investment, including:

- National Savings
  - Ordinary account interest
  - Certificates

- Government securities – exemption from capital gains tax

- PEPs

- TESSAs

- ISAs

- pensions

- unquoted shares (re-investment relief from capital gains tax)

- Friendly Societies

- employee share schemes.

Shareholder concessions are given by many companies on their shares.

CASE STUDIES

Brian buys a PEP
Brian has a windfall in the form of a legacy of £5,000. He decides to put this into an ISA, which will form part of his overall pension plan, but will also remain encashable should he need the money for any purpose. He has faith in the long term prospects for the economy generally, so he decides to invest in an index tracker ISA.

Charles
One of the sectors Charles has invested in is retail stores. He invests in Boots, and gets regular discount vouchers with his annual report package from the company. He also travels regularly to the continent, and buys the minimum 100 shares in Eurotunnel to get 30 per cent discounts on a number of journeys on Le Shuttle. He does not want to invest more than this in the company.

POINTS TO CONSIDER

1. Do you think that tax incentives should (or would) be enough to make you invest in a particular product?

2. What shareholder concessions might be of use to you?

10

Investing in Property

PROPERTY INVESTMENT

Land or property can be bought as an investment. It can provide both an income and a realistic opportunity to protect your capital. The main types of property investment are:

● commercial property (offices or shops)

● industrial units

● residential property

● holiday lettings.

As with any investment, the general rule of not putting all your eggs in one basket holds good. However, to invest in more than one property requires a substantial amount of money. If you have substantial funds, say in excess of £400,000, then it is possible to put together a good portfolio of investment properties.

Another feature of property investment is that it needs active management. If you have the time, interest, and knowledge, you could manage the property yourself. Alternatively, you could employ an agent to look after the management.

In general terms, property is a good long term investment, as it usually at least keeps up with inflation in the long term. However, there can be spells when the value stagnates, or even falls.

Commercial property

With the right circumstances, you could get between 10% and 14% return on commercial property. However, if you employ an agent to manage the property, do not forget that they will take their commission – usually 10% – from the rent. For shop premises, a prime trading position is one of the best attributes to obtain the best rent.

It is a good idea to get a lease drawn up by a solicitor or estate agent.

The lease should protect your interests by making it a full repairing and insuring lease – in other words, repairs and insurance are the tenant's responsibility. These days, leases can be between 7 years and 14 years duration, and generally provide for reviews of the rent every 3 years.

Commercial property is subject to the normal commercial risks associated with the economy generally. If there is a recession, or a downturn in retail sales generally, there is a risk of the bankruptcy of the tenant. In those circumstances, it may be difficult to re-let the property. At the same time, because of these conditions, it may also be difficult to sell the property at a realistic price.

Industrial units

The general circumstances for this type of investment are similar to those for commercial property. Returns of up to 15% can be expected. Again, if an agent manages the property, their commission will have to be taken into account.

This type of property is also, of course, subject to the risks associated with the cycle of economic activity – often, small manufacturers are among the first to be affected.

Residential property

The return on this type of property can be lower than commercial property – usually around 5%. Lettings are usually carried out on shorthold tenancies – either 6 months or a year.

When letting residential property, always get references on prospective tenants. There is always the nightmare of the 'tenant from hell' who does not pay the rent, and damages the property, causing much expense in putting it back in a good state of repair.

If you are letting a residential property furnished, you must comply with the 'Furniture and furnishings (Fire) (Safety) regulations'. This could prove expensive. There are also various laws governing these lettings, mainly the Landlord and Tenant Acts, and the Housing Act 1988. These acts give a great deal of protection to the tenant. If a tenant does not pay the rent, it can prove to be a long process to get them evicted – count on about 6 months. Usually, you can also count on having lost your rent for that 6 month period.

Make sure that bills for utilities, telephone *etc* are put into the tenant's name – you would not want to be left with demands for unpaid bills after the tenant has left.

Holiday lettings

Property to let for holidays would, of course, need to be in an area in which people want to take their holidays. The properties would also need regular attention to keep them up to acceptable standards for holiday letting. This means regular and frequent maintenance and redecoration. The furnishings should also be of a high standard, and comply with the regulations mentioned above.

Active management is vital, particular on change over days. An agent may be necessary to manage these properties – especially if the property is not geographically near you.

You can expect a return of 7%–8% on this type of property.

USING YOUR HOME

Your home is probably the largest single investment you will ever make. However, it is not just an investment like any other. A home is first and foremost a place to provide a safe and comfortable environment for you and your family to live in. It would be nonsense to buy a home because of the investment potential if you have six children, but the house only has one bedroom.

Whilst the value of your house may increase, it does not mean anything in real terms unless and until you can realise the value. The problem, of course, is that if you sold your house you would have to buy another house to live in. Unless you deliberately 'trade down', and buy a cheaper house, you would have to pay at least as much to buy another house, and also suffer the costs of buying, selling and removing.

FINANCING YOUR HOME

Because relatively few of us have the ready cash to buy a house, we have to raise some finance to buy a house. A loan that is secured on the property is called a **mortgage**. There are many suppliers of mortgage finance, of whom the commonest are banks and building societies.

When buying a house, you have to decide how much you can afford. This is determined not so much by the price of the house itself, but by how much deposit you can put down, and how much you can afford as regular repayments. There are several factors to bear in mind:

- loan to valuation
- income multiplier
- length of expected occupancy.

Loan to valuation

When you buy a house, and want a mortgage, the bank or building society will value it. The value they put on it may have no relationship at all to the price you pay for the house. It is done to determine how much security they have in the house. They must always look at the 'worst scenario'. This means that if you could not keep up the repayments, they would have to repossess the house and sell it to get back the money they loaned you. Therefore, the value is an important factor for them.

The amount you want to borrow is then considered as a percentage of the valuation figure. Thus, if they valued the house at £100,000, and you wanted to borrow £90,000, the loan to valuation is said to be 90 per cent. These days, most banks or building societies would not lend more than 95 per cent of the valuation. In the heady days of the mid 1980s, they were lending up to 100 per cent of the values, and too often these valuations were to prove optimistic when property prices crashed. This led to the 'negative equity' problem which has plagued many people's lives.

Normally, the loan to valuation affects the interest rate. A larger loan to valuation percentage means a higher rate of interest.

Income multiplier

This is another factor taken into consideration by banks and building societies. The amount you want to borrow is expressed as a 'multiplier' of your income. Thus, if your income is £15,000 per year, and you want to borrow £30,000, the income multiplier is said to be 2 times. Again, the loan is considered up to a maximum multiplier. The lender would not be happy about lending you more money than you could afford to repay.

A typical income multiplier for a single person might be 3.5 times income. For a couple it might be expressed as the higher of:

- 3.5 times first income plus 1 times second income, or
- 2.75 times joint income.

The highest income is considered as the first income.

Example
Husband's income £18,000 per year
Wife's income £10,000 per year.

3.5 times first income	=	£63.000
1 times second income	=	£10,000
Total		£73,000
or		
2.75 times joint income	=	£77,000

The maximum loan on this basis would be £77,000.

The income multiplier and the loan to valuation figures may not necessarily be the same, and the amount they would be willing to loan would be the lower of the two figures.

Length of expected occupancy

When considering how much you could afford, apart from taking into account the loan criteria, you should also consider how long you expect to be in the house. You may know that you will be moving on in a few years' time, either because your family is growing or because of a geographical move. That will obviously affect your decision about the house, whether you expect to do major improvements *etc*. It will also affect your decision about the term of the mortgage – *ie* the number of years over which it is to be repaid.

REPAYING THE MORTGAGE

Over time, the banks and building societies have developed many different ways of repaying the mortgage.

Repayment mortgage

The simplest is the repayment mortgage. This means that you make monthly repayments which include a part for the interest and a part for the capital. This is worked out according to the term of the loan and the interest rate prevailing when you borrow the money. Any subsequent changes in the interest rate mean that the monthly repayment has to be altered. Normally, the bank or building society would also require a life assurance protection policy to be taken out. This means that in the event of you dying before you have paid off the mortgage, the life assurance would pay off the balance owing. (The bank or building society are naturally uneasy about the prospect of having to repossess a house and throwing out a recently widowed person.)

Interest only mortgage

There are then various forms of 'interest only' repayment plans. This means that the monthly repayment is for interest only. The capital is not repaid monthly, but by means of a saving plan of some sort. The most usual are:

- endowment mortgages

- pension mortgages

- PEP mortgages.

Endowment mortgages

An endowment mortgage means that you take out an endowment life assurance policy for the term of the loan, and for the amount you borrowed. You make the normal premiums to the life assurance company. When the term of the mortgage is over, the life assurance policy matures, and the money is used to repay the capital of the mortgage. This also provides the life assurance protection to repay the mortgage if you die in the meantime.

Pension mortgages

A pension mortgage works on similar basis to an endowment mortgage. However, instead of taking out an endowment life assurance, you take out a personal pension policy. The earliest this could mature is age 50, so that the term of the mortgage could not end before that date. When the pension policy matures, you take the maximum tax free lump sum with which to repay the mortgage. This type of policy attracts tax relief at your top rate of tax, so you could, at present rates, get up to 40 per cent tax relief. However, only 25 per cent of the fund may be taken as a tax free lump sum, so that the funding needs to be at least four times the mortgage to ensure that the mortgage can be repaid.

PEP mortgages

A PEP mortgage is a scheme whereby, in addition to the interest payments monthly, you invest in a PEP investment. This then accumulates a fund to repay the mortgage at the end of the term. At the time of writing, this type of plan is in transition, because recently announced changes to tax free investments means that PEPs have not been available since April 1999.

Interest rates

Banks and building societies have been very competitive in recent years, and now offer a range of interest types, including discounts, cashbacks, and fixed interest rates.

Discounts are offered, some to first time buyers, and some as a simple incentive to persuade borrowers to change their mortgage lender. These discounts usually last for a fixed period, typically one, two or three years. The discounts are in terms of a cheaper interest rate for the period.

Cashbacks are also offered as an incentive. The cashback will typically be a percentage of the amount borrowed.

Both discounts and cashbacks are subject to penalties – *ie* repayment of the amount saved or repaid – if the mortgage is repaid within a certain time limit – usually five years.

Fixed interest rates are also quoted as an incentive. These are rates of interest that are guaranteed to stay the same for a given period. At the expiry of this period, the interest rate reverts to the normal variable interest rate. Some lenders offer fixed interest rates for a limited period as well as a cashback on the same loan.

REALISING THE VALUE IN YOUR HOME

You may have a large value locked up in your home, but how can you use it for your benefit? You could sell the house and use the capital to invest and generate income. However, this has the drawback that you need to find somewhere to live when you have sold your house. You could, of course, rent a home. This means, of course, that you have to be able to rent a home for less than the income your investment generates, otherwise you would be out of pocket over the deal.

You could also sell the house, buy a cheaper house, and invest the cash left over. This option could sometimes work if your children have left home, and you do not need such a big house. However, do not underestimate the costs of buying and selling, removing, and doing any necessary improvements to the new house.

Benefiting from home income plans

A number of companies specialise in providing an additional income from the value otherwise locked up in your home. These schemes are aimed at people in their retirement years. In the past, some companies offered schemes which were linked to investment bonds, and many people lost money on these types of schemes. They were not really appropriate to the market they were sold to, because they involved a higher degree of risk than was appropriate for the purpose.

The present home income plan market is made up of four main types of plan:

1. Shared appreciation mortgages

2. Roll-up loans

3. Home reversion schemes

4. Home income plans.

Shared appreciation mortgages
Under this scheme, you take out a mortgage secured on your property. You get a lump sum, and you can do what you like with it. The idea is

that you invest this to produce an income. You do not have to pay back any interest or capital, as long as you continue to own and live in the house. When you sell your house, or die, the mortgage loan is repaid, and in addition, a percentage (typically 75 per cent) of any increase in the value of the house since you took the loan is also repaid.

This type of scheme cannot be transferred from one house to another, so the loan must be repaid if you move house. This means that if you want to continue the scheme, a fresh loan application must be made each time you move house, incurring extra costs each time. There is no age limit to this scheme.

Roll-up loans

Under this scheme, you take out a mortgage secured on your property. You get a lump sum, and you can do with it what you like – again, the idea is that you invest it to produce an income. You do not have to make any interest or capital repayments, but the interest is 'rolled up' each year and added to the amount of your loan. The full amount is then repaid when you sell your house or when you die. In times of increasing house values, the increase in the value can keep pace with the increase in the amount of the loan.

Because of the compounding effect of rolling up the interest, you must be very cautious with this type of plan. The interest rates are variable for this type of plan, so that if interest rates increase, the compounding effect gathers pace. This also means that the loan to valuation for this type of plan should be very low – probably no higher than 20 per cent should be considered as safe. A further effect of this is that the longer the plan is likely to be in effect, the greater the risk of running up a large debt. Therefore, you should not consider this type of plan until at least age 70.

If the loan reaches a point where there is a danger of the loan catching up with the property value, you may be asked to start making repayments. It could force you into the position of having to sell the house to repay the loan.

Home reversion schemes

Under these schemes, you effectively sell your home, in whole or in part, to the reversion company. You then get either a lump sum or an annuity. You are guaranteed the security of living in the home for the rest of your life, either rent free or for only a nominal sum. Then when you sell your house or die, the reversion company gets the proportion of the sale proceeds. This proportion depends on the proportion you sold the company when you took out the scheme.

The amount of lump sum you would get is never the full market value of the house, because the reversion company has to make provision for you living there for the rest of your lives. Therefore, the older you are, the nearer will be the price you get to the market price.

Home income plans
Under this type of scheme, you take out a mortgage up to the maximum for which tax allowance is granted. The proceeds buy an annuity for the rest of your life. This gives you a monthly income, and from that income the interest on the mortgage is paid, and the balance is then paid to you.

You do not have to make any repayments of capital, and when you die or sell the property, the mortgage is repaid. However, because the annuity is unaffected, even if you sold the house and repaid the mortgage, the annuity payments would continue to be paid to you, and now they would be paid without the deduction of the mortgage interest.

Pausing to think

Whatever type of plan you are considering, you must stop to consider various things which could become problems. Things to take into account are:

● Are any valuation, survey fees *etc* reimbursed by the reversion company?

● Is the scheme transferable if you move house?

● Repairs and insurance – who is responsible?

● Will it affect any Social Security benefits you receive?

● What do your family think about it?

● What would happen if you took out the scheme as a single person and then married?

● What would happen if you took the scheme out as a married couple, and one of you died?

● What would happen if a family member or friend moved in to care for you or provide companionship?

● What is the minimum age?

● What is the maximum loan to valuation?

● What is the minimum property value?

● Is there any restriction on the type of property (*eg* house, flat, maisonette)?

CHECKLIST

● Financing your home purchase by mortgage. Consider:

    – loan to valuation

    – income multiplier

    – length of occupancy.

● Repayment types:

    – straight repayment mortgage

    – endowment mortgage

    – pension mortgage

    – PEP mortgage.

● Interest rates and incentives:

    – discounts

    – cashbacks

    – fixed rate

    – but beware penalties!

● Releasing the value in your home:

    – shared appreciation mortgage

    – roll-up loan

    – home reversion scheme

    – home income plan

    – try to anticipate problems!

CASE STUDIES

Alison opts for a repayment mortgage

Alison and her fiancé are saving to buy a house. They have not given much attention to the method of repayment, but they will probably start with a repayment mortgage. This is the simplest and cheapest method for the first few years, and they might be able to consider an alternative when they move house later on in their careers.

Charles picks a home income plan

Charles takes stock of the lifestyle he wants, and realises that he will need rather more income. He has no dependants, so he has no qualms about a home income plan. (The plan would mean that he might have less to leave in his estate.) He studies the plans and decides on a shared appreciation mortgage, as he has no plans to move house now. This provides a lump sum which he invests.

POINTS TO CONSIDER

1. Do you think that any type of endowment or pension mortgage is right for you in your circumstances? How does it fit in with your other plans and investments?

2. Do you feel that you are able to consider any of the home income plan type schemes?

3. Are there are any other people besides you who might be affected by a home income plan?

11

Using Life Assurance

UNDERSTANDING LIFE ASSURANCE

Whole life policies

Life assurance in its simplest and purest form is a form of protection. You pay a regular premium, each month or each year, and when you die, your dependants get a lump sum which will be of help to them. There has to be an 'insurable interest'. This means that you cannot just take out a life assurance policy on somebody unconnected to you – say, the President of the United States – and then collect a lump sum when he dies. It has to be somebody whose death would otherwise cause you loss. This is most commonly a family member, but it can be a key person in your business whose death would cause a financial loss.

This type of policy is known as a 'whole life' policy. Cover is provided throughout the life of the person insured, provided the premiums are paid. It can also cover the lives of two people, usually husband and wife. It is then known as a 'joint life' policy.

Term policies

Life assurance policies can be indefinite, or for a fixed term. A term policy would be taken out because the protection is only needed for a certain length of time – for example, during the period of repaying a mortgage.

A level term policy is one in which the amount of the cover stays the same for the whole term of the policy. A decreasing term policy is one in which the cover decreases year by year. This type of policy is often used in conjunction with repayment mortgages, where the balance on the mortgage account decreases each year, and the policy provides cover which broadly matches the decreasing balance.

Endowment policies

However, a development of the simple 'protection' type policy was the endowment policy. This added a savings element to the protection element. The premiums are of course higher for this sort of policy. But the key feature is that they cover a definite period (the term), during which your life would be insured for a certain sum, but at the end of the term (known as the maturity), if you are still alive, you receive a lump sum. The most common type of endowment policy is a **with profits** policy. This means that the amount paid in each year is invested by the insurance company, and part of the profits each year are added to the value of the policy which is paid out at maturity.

This is done by the insurance company declaring **reversionary bonuses** each year which are added to the value of the policy. These bonuses cannot be deducted once they have been added. Reversionary bonuses do not tend to suffer the extremes of fluctuations that other 'unit linked' policies do. This is because the bonuses are subject to a 'rolling average' adjustment. This ensures that large fluctuations in the value of the underlying investments are smoothed out, and a more level bonus is added each year. Then, at the maturity, a 'terminal bonus' is added. The terminal bonus is not guaranteed. The terminal bonus tends to fluctuate more than the reversionary bonus, because it is more affected by the actual increase or decrease in the value of the underlying investments of the particular year in which the terminal bonus is added.

Unitised policies

Some endowment policies are **unitised**. That means that the premiums buy units in the with profits fund. The unit prices increase as the annual bonus is added on a daily basis. At the maturity of the policy, the value of the units plus a terminal bonus is paid out.

Endowment mortgages

A relatively recent development has been the combination of endowment policies with mortgages. The amount of the mortgage is covered by taking out an endowment policy for the term of the mortgage. Then, the repayments to the mortgage lender are of interest only. At the maturity of the endowment policy the mortgage is paid off with the maturity proceeds of the policy. The protection element is provided by this policy as well as the investment element.

In practice, these policies have been taken out with the prospect of the maturity sum covering not just the repayment of the mortgage but also an additional sum. However, these policies are at the mercy of the bonus rates declared. In recent years, some shorter term policies have not always covered the full outstanding amount of the policy, because the bonuses have been insufficient.

Bonds

Another relatively recent development has been the **insurance bond.** This is in effect a single premium endowment assurance policy, if it has a fixed term. If it continues until death, then it is an open ended whole of life policy. The fixed term is often five or ten years.

Income bonds
In return for a single premium paid 'up front' you receive a fixed income each year, and the return of the premium, sometimes with some increase added, at the end of the term. Because of tax regulations, these can be advantageous in certain cases.

Capital growth bonds
The single premium is paid 'up front', but instead of the income being paid out, it 'rolls up' in the policy to provide a larger sum on maturity.

Commission
As with all insurance policies, if they are sold to you by tied agents or independent advisers, they may be subject to commission being paid. The effect of this is particularly noticeable with bonds. The initial commission may mean that if you wanted to withdraw the money in the early years, you might suffer a loss. Always check this before you invest.

Trading endowment policies
In the past, if you found that you could not keep up the premiums on endowment policies, the only thing to do was to surrender them to the insurance company. You could get back a certain amount, depending on the number of years you had been paying the premiums. However, the amount would always be at a large discount to the true value of your fund.

In recent years, a market has grown up in **traded endowment policies**. This means that instead of simply surrendering your endowment policy to the insurance company, you could sell them to another person who would continue to pay the premiums, and then collect the funds at maturity. In general, this method produces a larger amount than surrendering the policy.

Buying traded endowment policies (TEPs) has also been seen as an investment tool. A person buying such a policy takes over the liability for the remaining premiums, and the policy continues on the life of the original person who sold the policy. The amount paid for the policy depends on several factors, of which the most obvious is the remaining time left until maturity. The earlier death of the original life would of course mean an earlier maturity.

This type of investment is fairly complex, and needs the advice of the market makers, of whom several specialise in this area. However, it is a relatively low risk investment, since the minimum value of the policy usually corresponds very closely to the purchase price and premiums paid. Then at maturity a relatively large amount is added as terminal bonus.

Once again, however, the amount of the final benefit is at the mercy of the bonuses. In recent years, annual bonuses have fallen. In some cases, the terminal bonus is also lower, and the overall return for a purchased endowment policy could be disappointing.

CHECKLIST

● Use whole of life and term assurance for protection.

● Endowment policies, sometimes connected to mortgages, can be a good investment over the long term.

● Bonds can be tax efficient in some cases.

● Traded endowment policies can give you more money if you need to surrender the policy, but beware of buying – the bonuses may be disappointing in the short term.

CASE STUDY

Alison considers an endowment mortgage

Alison considers the benefits of an endowment mortgage when she gets a mortgage. She likes the idea of saving in this way. As she is still fairly young, the cost of this type of policy is not great. She has also considered the idea of a pension mortgage, but rejected this. She is not sure at this stage of how long her working life might be, and how long she might take out of a career to raise a family.

POINTS TO CONSIDER

1. Have you worked out how much you need to insure your life for? Have you regularly reviewed it?

2. Do you know if you would benefit from the tax treatment of bonds?

3. If you are taking out a mortgage, do you understand the difference between a repayment mortgage and an endowment mortgage?

12

Being Unconventional

THINKING LATERALLY

There are a number of investment opportunities which are not 'conventional'. Many people fight shy of these, simply because they are unconventional. The real problem is a lack of understanding.

Here is the tenth Commandment of Saving and Investing:

Do not invest in anything unless you understand it.

Some years ago, a large pension fund raised a few eyebrows because it invested in an 'old master' painting. In the event, it actually made a good profit for the pension fund. If you are thinking of being unorthodox in your investments, then:

- make sure you understand the thing you are investing in, and
- evaluate the risk factor.

There are many sorts of investments which could be considered as unorthodox, and we will look at the following:

- ethical investments
- collectibles, including wines
- commodities
- dealing in stocks and shares
- derivatives
- spread betting.

ETHICAL INVESTMENTS

There is now a large choice of **ethical funds**. These offer the investor with a conscience the chance to put his money where his mouth is. There are two main types of ethical investment – positive and negative.

Positive investments

Positive investments channel money into companies that promote a certain ethical or 'green' agenda. These include:

- energy and resource conservation
- recycling
- renewable energy
- pollution control
- free range foods
- sustainable agriculture and forestry
- minimising waste
- environmental technology
- public transport
- fair trade with third world countries.

Negative investments

Negative investments concentrate on avoiding companies which are involved in things such as:

- tobacco
- alcohol
- arms trade
- exploitation of third world countries
- heavy pollution
- animal testing
- pornography
- environmental damage.

Many PEPs and unit trusts now allow you to choose the right type of ethical investment to suit your preferences. The good news is that most of the ethical funds perform at least as well as other funds in the same sector of the market. A recent survey of the FTSE 100 companies showed that the 'greenest' and 'most ethical' companies performed better than those at the other of the scale. You do not need to suffer financially in order to exercise your conscience.

If you are going to invest ethically, the one question you need to ask yourself is – Does it make sense to invest only part of my money in ethical investments? The logic of ethical investment is that all your money should be invested ethically if that is where your scruples lead you. To put it another way, ethical investment is not something you can 'dabble' in. If you only put a token amount in ethical investments, then the rest of your money is going into non-ethical investments.

Ethical banks and building societies

Saving with a bank or building society can also be done ethically. The main opportunities here are with the Co-operative bank, the Ecology building society, and Triodos bank.

- The Co-operative bank has two million customers, and does not deal with repressive regimes overseas, the fur trade, tobacco producers, field sports, or animal experiments for cosmetics.

- The Ecology building society specialises in lending money for socially responsible housing projects.

- The Triodos bank is a Dutch bank that has been in the UK since 1995. It invests in projects which add social or environmental value.

Some 'ethical' banks or building societies offer accounts which pay interest equivalent to the rate of inflation, and pass on profits to worthy causes. They usually also offer TESSAs.

Finally – remember the Eleventh commandment of Saving and Investing:

Ethical investments are not necessarily low risk.

COLLECTIBLES

Most people have in childhood collected things – stamps, football programmes, teddy bears, dolls – in fact almost anything. Many collectors take these things seriously into adult life, and other sorts of collections are often only developed in adult life. These include such things as fine wines, antiquarian books, paintings, *etc.*

There are many sorts of collections you could make if you have a mind to. Some which have established markets are:

- political memorabilia
- antique greeting cards
- sporting equipment and memorabilia
- oriental ceramics
- carpets and rugs
- furniture
- toys
- film posters
- garden statuary
- stuffed animals and fish.

This is by no means a complete list, but it gives an idea of the range of things which could make collections, and for which a market exists.

To make an investment out of a collection does not take much apart from a serious dedication to it. However, collections are usually made primarily for pleasure. The investment potential should only be secondary. There are three main things to bear in mind when considering collectibles.

Knowing your subject

Most collections come about through an interest in the items – often the interest is kindled as a child, and grows in adult life. In order to make a collection into a serious investment, you should know your subject well. It is no use collecting, say, fine wines if you do not know which ones will improve when they are laid down, and which ones will increase in value. But do not be put off by a mystique about any subject. If something interests you, learn more about it. You can become an enthusiast, and even an expert about your pet subject. Some collections may be built up by spending much time at car boot sales or the like. Others may need serious buying at auctions or specialist shops.

Keeping them safe

The one thing that is different about collectibles is that they have an actual physical existence. That means that they need to be kept somewhere. Some items may need special storage conditions, such as a cool wine cellar. Some items, such as pictures, may need to be displayed and lit to be properly appreciated. Some items are even of such importance that they are loaned to a local or national museum for display. Many items will be of some value, and will therefore need to be protected. This may mean special anti-burglary precautions, and for any serious collection, your normal household insurance will probably not cover it for loss or damage. You will probably have to incur extra cost in insuring it specifically.

Realising their value

Collections suffer from one obvious disadvantage – they do not produce an income. Therefore, in order to benefit from them in a financial sense, you will have to realise their value in some way. This could mean having to part with something you have become attached to. Bear this in mind at the outset.

COMMODITIES

Commodities include products such as coffee, cocoa, metals of all sorts – in fact, the raw materials that are used in industrial and food production. Because many of these come from abroad, and the process time to get them to the finished products can be considerable, the businesses that buy and sell them like to hedge the prices. This has led to markets growing up in which investors and speculators can trade in the future prices of these commodities.

The dealings take place in highly regulated environments. Outside investors can only deal through brokers, and are essentially taking a gamble on the future prices of the commodities traded in. The amounts needed to trade in these futures are not inconsiderable, and it is a high risk area.

PLAYING THE STOCK MARKET

Anyone who has a portfolio of stocks and shares does a certain amount of buying and selling of shares. However, it is possible to make the buying and selling of stocks and shares a separate speculative activity. It is not so much the yield from dividends that is sought, but the profits to be had from trading the shares. If you do this consistently, the Inland Revenue can and will treat you as being in business as a share trader.

This form of speculation can be high risk. If you have enough money you can spread the risk by holding many different stocks and shares. Speculators are trying to anticipate the movement of the markets. This can mean spending much time reading the reports of analysts about various companies, or generally keeping up to date with market news (and market rumours). Not all speculators are short term dealers. Some take a long term view, and their stocks or shares are held a long time before being sold. To that extent, they are acting in the same way as traditional investors.

Charting for pleasure and profit

'Chartists' are people who look for patterns in the price movements of shares. These patterns are seen easily in charts or graphs of the price movements. The peaks and troughs form patterns which can be related to past experience to indicate that a price is about to peak, or has bottomed out. This indicates when to buy or sell.

Chartists are therefore not concerned so much with the details of the economic reality of the company represented by those shares, but the actions of a wide spread of investors. Perhaps the most well known expression of this is the Elliott Wave Principle, first propounded by R N Elliott in 1934, in the United States. It is based on the patterns created by graphs of price movements. Although this may seem esoteric, the 'rules' derived from it have proved reliable. They do not claim to be able to predict the future, but to provide a structure for analysis of markets.

If you have the time to devote to it, and a mathematical bent, it can be an interesting pursuit as well as an investment opportunity. Always remember, however, that this is still in the realms of speculative investment.

Day Trading

Another form of speculative investment is day trading. This involves buying and selling investments on the same day, in the hope of making a profit. Because of the dealing charges, there has to be a large movement in the price of the investment to make this worthwhile. However, because trading all takes place on the same day, you do not need capital to do it.

Never lose sight of the precarious nature of this type of trading. It is reckoned that about 70% of those carrying out day trading make losses.

DERIVATIVES

These are also known as **Options**, but the term 'derivatives' can also embrace other things such as futures, contracts for differences, swaps, *etc.* They appear complicated, and certainly, it would normally be more sophisticated investors who deal in these. Remember – do not invest in anything unless you understand it. The essence of derivatives is that you have the opportunity to benefit (or lose) from an underlying 'position' (such as the movement in the price of a share) without complete exposure to that position. In plain language that means you can benefit from an increase in a share price without actually owning the shares.

The simplest form of derivative is the option. These are agreements by which you pay a price (known as the option premium) for the right to buy or sell shares at a fixed price within a certain time scale. These agreements also limit the number of shares to be traded under the agreement.

If you do not exercise your option within the time scale, you have lost the rights under that agreement. The person to whom you paid the premium keeps the money. However, if you do exercise your right, the person to whom you paid the premium must fulfil their side of the bargain.

Types of option:
The types of option are:

- calls – this gives the right to buy the shares

- puts – this gives the right to sell the shares

- doubles – this gives the right either to buy or sell, but not both.

This form of trading is recognised on the London Stock Exchange and is called 'London's Traditional Options Market'. Shares in any company quoted on the London Stock Exchange may be the subject of a traditional options contract.

Traded options
There is another market dealing in 'traded options'. This is a separate market in which the options are for fixed numbers of shares, with fixed expiry patterns, and a fixed scale of exercise prices. On the traded options market, the options themselves can be traded, rather than the underlying shares, and the range of shares on which options are traded is rather more limited than on the London Stock Exchange.

Options could be considered low to medium risk in the sense that the only money at risk is the money you have paid for the option premium. This is only a fraction of the cost of holding the actual shares. However, the option premium itself is a high risk item, since the loss could be 100 per cent.

SPREAD BETTING
As the name implies, this is a form of gambling, and the firms which operate this are registered as bookmakers. The risk factor is therefore self-evident. In fact, the main 'player' in this field, City Index Ltd, deals in sports spread betting as well as financial spread betting. Spread betting may be done on stock market indices from all over the world, individual share prices, government bond prices, interest rates, currency

rates of exchange, precious metals, commodities, and traded options. All bets are made on future movements of the items.

Examples

The way it works is this, using as an example spread betting on the FTSE 100 index. You ask for a bet on the index figure in, say, three months' time. The bookmaker will give you a range (which is the 'spread'). Let us say the spread they give is 5450 to 5500. If you think the index will be lower than 5450, you 'sell' points at whatever you decide to stake per point, say, £10 per point. If you think the index will be higher than 5500, you 'buy' points. Then, at the date of the bet quote – *ie* three months' time in this example – if the price is 5400, and you have 'sold' points, then you have won 50 points. Multiply this by your stake to arrive at your winnings. In this example it would £500. However, if the index had gone up to 5550, and you had sold points, you have then lost 100 points. This would have meant a loss of £1,000.

You do not have to wait the full term to cash in your winnings, or take your losses. You can 'close' the bet at any time. Let us look at another example.

You have a quote for the FTSE index three months ahead of 5450 to 5500. You buy points at £10 per point. At the end of two months, the index daily quote is down to 5400 to 5440. You are currently losing 100 points. You decide to cut your losses at this time. You do this by selling at the daily quote. You have then limited your losses to 100 points at £10 per point.

This works in a similar way if you are winning at the two month stage, and wish to take your winnings now, because you do not think the movement in the index will continue.

There are other refinements such as placing a limit on the losses you can make, or rolling over a bet into the next three month term.

Although spread betting is a gamble, there is a circumstance in which it can be used as a hedge on investment portfolios. If you want to hedge against the possibility of the value of your portfolio of shares falling drastically, you can take out a 'sell' bet which would give you winnings if the value falls, and could offset the losses on your shares.

CHECKLIST

● Ethical investments:
  – positive or negative
  – PEPS or unit trusts
  – bank or building societies
  – not necessarily low risk.

- Collectibles:
    - not just an investment, but also a leisure pursuit
    - know your subject
    - keep the collection safe
    - be prepared to realise their value.
- Commodities:
    - speculation based on future pricing
    - high risk.
- Dealing in stocks and shares:
    - speculative trading
    - high risk.
- Derivatives:
    - options can be call, put or double
    - London's traditional options market – part of the London Stock Exchange.
- Spread betting:
    - really a form of gambling
    - based on forecasting forward prices on stock markets
    - can be used as a hedge against losses.

CASE STUDY

Max learns the hard way

Max is a sophisticated and wealthy investor. He is willing to put aside a relatively small part of his wealth to try some speculative forms of investment. He dabbles in options and commodity trading. However, because he is only dabbling, he loses heavily, and decides to stick to the things he understands better. Although he has lost money, he is wealthy, and had mentally resigned himself to the fact that he could lose the money before he even started.

POINTS TO CONSIDER

1. Are you in a position to set aside some wealth for more unorthodox investments?

2. Do you feel strongly enough about any ethical issues that you would invest in them?

3. Do you agree that you should invest 'all or nothing' in ethical investments?

4. Do you have any interest which could form the basis of a collection, and if so, could this form part of your investment strategy?

13

Planning Beyond the Grave

PASSING YOUR WEALTH TO THE NEXT GENERATION

The main purpose of planning your savings is to enable them to work for you to give you the sort of lifestyle you want. However, we would all like to be able to pass on something to our children, and our children's children. How can you make sure it does all pass on to them?

The main threat to passing on all of your wealth to your dependants is inheritance tax. Anything passing to your surviving spouse is free of inheritance tax, but beyond that, anything above £234,000 suffers tax at 40 per cent. It is not difficult to pass on an estate worth more than £234,000, so you should look at this problem. The earlier you take some action, the more effective it is likely to be.

Making gifts

If you make outright gifts during your lifetime, they are known as 'potentially exempt transfers' (PETs). If you survive seven years after making the gift, they fall out of your estate for inheritance tax purposes. However, there is a tapering relief if you should die within seven years of making a gift. Gifts within seven years of death are taxed using the following taper scale:

Years between gift and death	Percentage of full charge
0 – 3	100
3 – 4	80
4 – 5	60
5 – 6	40
6 – 7	20

In addition to PETs, you may give away other gifts which are exempt from the Inheritance Tax charge as follows:

- Annual exemption £3,000 for all gifts, and in addition –

- Small gifts to any person £250, and

- Marriage gifts:
  - made by parents to their children £5,000
  - made by grandparents (or great grandparents) to their grand-children (or great grandchildren) £2,500
  - made by husband or wife to their spouse £2,500
  - made by any other person £1,000.

Staying out of the workhouse

It is all very well making gifts so that you reduce the amount of inheritance tax that your relatives pay. However, you should of course not give away so much that you leave yourself short. In the past, some insurance plans catered for this by making gifts into trusts for the benefit of your dependants, but until your death, the money in those trusts generated an income which you benefited from. These have now been abolished. A gift must be an outright gift to be a PET. There must be no 'reservation of title or benefit'.

The general rule is, therefore, only give away what you can actually afford to do without.

Skipping generations

Your children may already be well provided for, and you may consider that you want to pass some money directly to your grandchildren. This could ease your children's inheritance tax problems also. Be prepared to review your will and alter it periodically if necessary.

Using insurance

Because there is no charge to inheritance tax on transfers between husband and wife, you need not worry about how much you leave your spouse. The only charge to inheritance tax is on the second death. Therefore, a life assurance policy on joint lives, which pays out on the second death, can be a useful way of providing for inheritance tax. The premium would normally be cheaper on this type of policy, because the risk insured against is the second death, and that is more likely to be much later. The policy, however, must be written so that the proceeds are in trust for the ultimate beneficiaries.

This can be a good solution to providing for inheritance tax on its own, without any need to resort to making gifts or restructuring investments.

Using trusts

A trust is a legal way in which a sum of money or an asset is set apart. It is given to a **trustee**, who has a legal constraint to use the money or asset in the way in which the person giving it determines. The person who gives the money or asset is called the **settlor**. The trust assets are usually to be applied for the benefit of a person or persons (the beneficiaries) with successive entitlements when the beneficiary dies. The settlor can also be the trustee, or one of several trustees.

A trust can protect the assets from the effects of divorce, creditors, predatory step-relatives *etc*. It can also provide for the asset to be protected and accumulated when the beneficiaries are young. It can, therefore be a very useful and flexible tool. However, you must always get professional advice in drawing up a trust. Incorrect wording of a trust can have adverse consequences.

Main types of trust
The main uses of trusts for inheritance tax planning are as follows.

An **interest in possession** trust is a potentially exempt transfer. This sort of trust is one whereby the beneficiary has a right to the enjoyment of the income from the trust assets during his or her lifetime. On the death of the beneficiary or some other event specified in the trust, the right to the income or the outright ownership of the assets passes to another person or persons.

An **accumulation and maintenance** trust is also a potentially exempt transfer. This sort of trust is normally set up for children. The trust income must be accumulated for the benefit of the beneficiary at any age between 18 and 25. The trustees have the power to distribute income from the trust for the education or maintenance of the beneficiary before the final date. To qualify for the relief, the trust must have beneficiaries who are all grandchildren of a common grandparent and who are all under the age of 25. It must also ensure that the beneficiaries become entitled to the income or the capital of the trust when they reach 25 at the latest, and must accumulate any income not used for education or maintenance of the beneficiary.

A trust for the benefit of a mentally or physically disabled person is also a potentially exempt transfer.

Making your will
It is said that many more spouses are the victims of intestacy than of divorce. If you fail to make a will, or it becomes out of date, it could mean that more of your estate goes to pay tax than you wanted. Therefore:

● make a will

● review it regularly

● take professional advice.

CHECKLIST

- Ensure that your will expresses your intentions about your estate.

- Review it regularly.

- Think about using up your gift allowances, but only if you can afford it comfortably.

- Take advice about trusts, and life assurance policies, if you think these may be relevant.

CASE STUDIES

Brian decides to make a will

Brian has not thought about a will before, so he and his wife make an appointment with a solicitor to make their wills. His estate does not yet give any cause for deeper planning.

Max takes professional advice

When Max makes an inventory of his assets, he realises that his estate could be liable for a lot of inheritance tax, particularly if he and his wife both died at the same time. He therefore consults his accountant and his solicitor. He revises his will to create an accumulation and maintenance trust for his grandchildren. He also provides in his will for legacies for his children and grandchildren, making sure, however, that he provides more than enough for his wife if he should die before her.

He also feels that he could fund a life assurance policy on the joint lives of himself and his wife, written in trust for his children, to provide for the inheritance tax that would be payable.

POINTS TO CONSIDER

1. Have you totted up the value of your estate? Will you be liable for inheritance tax?

2. Have you considered or reconsidered your will? Does it express what you want to happen to your money when you die?

3. Could you make use of life assurance or trusts to reduce your estate's liability to inheritance tax?

14

Taking Advice

WHO ARE THE ADVISERS?

There are many 'financial advisers' around at the present, and their public image is probably similar to that of estate agents in the 1980s. So should you look for professional advice? Do they have any insights or inside information?

Independent advisers

Independent advisers can advise on any company's products. Since the Financial Services Act 1986, it is an offence to give investment advice without the proper authorisation. Most independent advisers are registered with the PIA (Personal Investment Authority). This is one of several regulatory bodies under the overall umbrella of the FSA (Financial Services Authority). This is to provide the public protection necessary to keep the public from sharp practices. Advisers registered with one of the bodies must pay annual fees which cover inspection visits, and they must also provide professional indemnity insurance cover.

Tied agents

Tied agents are representatives of one company. They can only advise on the products of that company. Most of the banks and building societies are in this position, and their literature will state this fact. This does not necessarily mean that they offer worse advice than an independent adviser, but their scope is limited.

Knowing how they are remunerated

Both independent advisers and tied agents can be remunerated by commission. Independent advisers can also charge a fee, usually based on an hourly rate. It is worth asking the adviser what his or her fees would be, and then asking how this would compare with the commission they would get on the investment. Although the fee may seem high (it would be typical, for example, to see a fee of £500–£600 for arranging a pension) that may be less than the commission. The main point of this is that the commission comes out of your initial investment – either in a pension, endowment policy, unit trusts, *etc*. It is not unusual for the commission on an endowment policy to account for over 85 per cent of the first year's premiums.

Therefore, if the adviser is willing to work for a fee, the commission is waived, and more of your original money goes into the actual investment.

Knowing what to ask

The National Consumers Council recommends that you ask the following questions of an adviser before signing up for any investment:

1. Are you able to give advice on a range of companies, or are you tied to one company?

2. What happens if I have to drop out early? What are the penalties?

3. Can I vary my payments on a regular investment if I have to?

4. If there are several alternatives which suit my needs, what is the commission you would get from each one?

5. What proportion of my investment goes on charges? How does this compare with other products?

6. What is the 'worst case scenario' that could happen to this product?

7. What happens if the product fails or the company goes bust?

8. Do you know of any other products on the market that are as good as or better than the one you are recommending?

9. Can you show me any independent information on how this product compares with others on the market?

DECIDING WHETHER TO USE AN ADVISER (AND WHICH ONE)

This chapter so far may be interpreted as telling you not to use an adviser because of their fees or commission. However, advisers can help you choose the right product. The result of taking their advice, even after taking into account their commission, can be considerably better than going it alone.

Some insurance and pension companies market their products on the strength of not paying commission to intermediaries. In general, many of these companies do have a sales force whom they pay well, and their expenses can be as much as companies that do pay commission to intermediaries.

If you are confident that:

● you understand all the issues involved, and

● you have the time to investigate all the alternatives on offer, and

● you can judge the technical qualities of the product

then you can go ahead and arrange your own investments or pension.

If however, you feel that you need advice, then to whom do you turn? The best advice is to get a personal recommendation. Ask around your friends or relatives. If they have someone they can trust, that is the best recommendation. If you cannot find one that way, look around locally, or through your *Yellow Pages*. Make an appointment, and explain your situation. A reputable adviser will:

● have to comply with strict regulatory requirements

● look at the whole of your circumstances, not just the immediate topic

● not try to pressure you into a quick decision.

If you feel you can trust the person, and have confidence in him or her, then go ahead with his or her recommendations.

The twelfth Commandment of Saving and Investment:

> Never let yourself be rushed or pressured into an investment.

CHECKLIST

● Find out whether an adviser is independent or tied.

● Ask if the remuneration is by fee or commission.

● Ask all the right questions.

● Try to get a recommendation.

● Only use someone you feel happy with.

CASE STUDY

Charles chooses an adviser carefully

Charles senses that he has gone about his financial matters in a piece-meal way, and he feels that he could benefit from an overall review of his finances, particularly investments and savings. His brother-in-law recommends an independent adviser, but Charles feels after the first interview that he would not get along with him on a personal basis. He therefore asks around again, and a friend recommends another adviser. This time Charles decides he can put his confidence in him. He makes a further appointment, and gathers all his financial information together for the next meeting. The adviser suggests that Charles's wife participate in the interview.

After a couple of interviews, Charles and his wife decide on some changes to the basic structure of their finances.

POINTS TO CONSIDER

1. Do you feel that a tied agent would not necessarily give as good advice as an independent adviser? Why?

15

Using the Internet

ACCESSING INFORMATION

There are many providers of financial information such as newspapers on the Internet. Many web sites are accessible free. Among the newspapers and journals on the Internet are:

- Investors Chronicle – at www.investorschronicle.co.uk

- Financial Times – at www.ft.co.uk

- The Economist – at www.economist.com

- Financial Mail Online – at www.thisismoney.co.uk

- The Times (Money Section) – at www.times-money.co.uk

- The Electronic Telegraph – at www.telegraph.co.uk

These sites give a host of financial information, articles and advice, aimed at UK citizens. This is an important feature, since many other sites are US based.

There are now many magazines (called 'ezines') which are published only on the Internet. Amongst these, the following offer financial information.

- Excite Money channel – at www.excite.co.uk

- Interactive Investor International – at www.iii.co.uk

- Moneyworld – at www.moneyworld.co.uk

- The Motley Fool – at www.fool.co.uk

- UK-Invest – at www.uk-invest.com

- Yahoo! Finance – at http://finance.uk.yahoo.com

Then there are sites which act as a directory of financial web sites. These include:

- Financial Information Net Directory – at www.find.co.uk

- Money Shop – at www.moneyshop.co.uk

Share Prices

Other services are offered by various providers in return for a subscription fee. These services are, of course, more than you can get free of charge. For example, Electronic Share Information at www.esi.co.uk offer a subscription service to get share prices in real time. Other services, such as the magazines quoted above, give you share prices updated every 15 minutes, but after a 20 minute delay. Several companies offer share dealing on their subscription service. Amongst the Internet dealing companies are:

- Barclays Stockbrokers – at www.barclays-stockbrokers.co.uk

- E*Trade UK Ltd.-at www.etrade.co.uk

- FasTrade – at www.fastrade.co.uk

- Xest – at www.xest.com

Surfing the Web

If you are willing to put in the time, you can also use Internet to survey all the current information on whatever subject you want. For example, if you are looking for the best rate of interest on a building society account, you could access all their web sites and compare rates. If you need the exercise, you could of course walk round the streets of the nearest big town – but then, you might miss some. The same approach could be used for insurance quotes, bank loans, mortgages, *etc*.

The Inland Revenue are online at www.inlandrevenue.gov.uk to give information and help about tax matters, guided by that cuddly cartoon character, Hector the Inspector.

GETTING ADVICE

Some sites offer advice rather than simple information. Some such sites are:

- Your Mortgage – at www.yourmortgage.co.uk/ This gives advice about the best choices in various mortgage products, such as remortgages, discount mortgages, fixed interest mortgages, *etc.*

- Carpetbaggers – at www.carpetbagger.com gives advice about the most likely building societies and insurance companies to demutualise and give shares or other bonuses to their savers.

- Which? Online – at www.which.net gives advice on many aspects of finance, amongst other things, including their famous 'best buy' tables.

- FT Your Money – at www.ftyourmoney.com. This site is run by Financial Times, and gives a host of information and advice. Much of the advice is slanted towards people in certain circumstances, such as Young and single, Middle Aged, with children approaching further education, pre-retirement, *etc.*

- Moneyweb – at www.moneyweb.co.uk. This site is run by a man who describes himself as 'a financial services insider for many years, but is now free to tell it as it is'.

- Tipsheets – at www.tipsheets.co.uk. This gives you access to all the UK investment newsletters issued by firms regulated by the Personal Investment Authority.

BANKING ON THE NET

Online banking is possible, and many banks now offer this facility. It can be particularly useful to people who are on the move. As with 'ordinary' banking, security is a vital element of online banking. A system of code words and encryption ensures security to a high degree – so much so, that the courts already recognise the legality of 'digital signatures'.

Many banks now offer a free Internet Access Service to their customers, as an incentive. One bank (Egg – the banking arm of Prudential) offers an Internet only savings account.

INVESTING ON THE NET

Practically all the large (and some not so large) investment and insurance companies have a web site. These sites may include much information and extra 'goodies', but their main purpose is to sell their products to you. Many sites allow you to apply for their products online, and almost all keep the prices of their investments posted on their sites.

KEEPING YOUR WITS ABOUT YOU

Many web sites are in effect advertising spaces. The competition for your financial business is hot, and the sites offer a certain amount of information, but not always the crucial figures you want. Their approach is to get as much information about you as possible, including your telephone number, so that their salesman can arrange a one – to – one interview and try to sell you something. Beware of what information you give out on the Internet!

JOINING A CYBER INVESTORS CLUB

Many of the general financial information services offer a bulletin board facility. This has proved to be a sort of 'investors club' where investors exchange information or rumours about topics related to investing. One particular site calls itself a 'cyber pub', where you can meet friends and discuss information and opinions about financial matters – with or without a pint in your hand. As well as the chat forum, there will also soon be courses for the serious student. You can find all this at the Bull and Bear – at www.bullandbear.com

CHECKLIST

Use the Internet for –

● Information

● Advice

● Banking

● Dealing.

But beware of the sharks out there!

CASE STUDY

Charles falls for the Internet

Charles has a computer, and has just become connected to the Internet. He decides to use it to become updated quicker about financial matters. After a few months, his wife complains that he has become addicted!

Appendix I
Summary of Investment
and Saving Opportunities

This appendix gives a summary of the various types of opportunities available, with comments on the risk profile and other features.

ORDINARY SHARES (EQUITIES)

Risk profile
Medium. Short term higher risk, but long term lower risk.

Income
Fluctuating. Depends on performance of the company. Good quality shares stand a realistic chance of the income increasing each year in line with inflation.

Capital protection
In the short term, capital value can fluctuate. Over the long term, equities have produced the best record of any form of investment of capital growth, and have at least kept pace with inflation.

Tax breaks
None.

Simplicity
You should have some degree of confidence and understanding of the stock market. You should not invest in this way if you would worry about the ups and downs of the share prices.

UNIT TRUSTS

Income trusts
Risk profile
Low to medium. The collective nature of the investment reduces risk exposure.

Income
Fluctuating. Stands a realistic chance of increasing each year at least in line with inflation.

Capital protection
In the short term, the capital value can fluctuate. In the long term, reasonably good chance of keeping up with inflation.

Tax breaks
Most unit trust groups have ISAs.

Simplicity
If purchased and left, can be the source of a regular, increasing income. Should be seen as a long term investment.

Growth funds
Risk profile
Slightly higher than income funds of unit trusts. The fund is usually invested in smaller companies with greater growth potential. This implies a slightly higher risk element.

Income
Usually low, fluctuating.

Capital protection
Good. The funds are designed for capital growth.

Simplicity
Needs to be purchased and left to grow. Good for situations where the investor does not need income, but may want it later.

High income funds
Risk profile
Slightly lower than income funds or unit trusts. They have a higher proportion invested in fixed interest investments.

Income
As the name suggests, higher immediate income than income funds. But not such good prospects for income growth.

Capital protection
Low chance of significant growth of the capital value.

Simplicity
Needs to be purchased and left to produce higher than average income.

Geographical funds
Risk profile
Medium to high risk. Generally higher risk than general income funds. They tend to concentrate on a geographical area which could be subject to wider fluctuation than general funds.

Income
Usually quite low.

Capital protection
More risky and therefore not such good prospects of protection.

Simplicity
Needs understanding and confidence in higher risk areas.

Ethical funds
These can be quite varied, and do not easily fit into a category for risk, income, capital protection or simplicity.

Smaller company funds
Risk profile
High risk.

Income
Usually quite low.

Capital protection
Can be very profitable, but can be disastrous.

Simplicity
Needs a strong nerve, and willingness to risk exposure.

Tracker funds
Risk profile
Low to medium risk. Lower risk than normal income fund. The investment is in the whole range of the chosen index.

Income
Lower than an income fund. Good chance of increasing income.

Capital protection
Good.

Simplicity
Very simple concept. Low management activity needed, keeping costs down.

Gilt and fixed interest funds
Risk profile
Low risk.

Income
Fixed income, usually higher rate than income funds. No prospects of increasing income.

Capital protection
Poor chance of capital appreciation to any great extent.

Simplicity
Easy to understand.

INVESTMENT TRUSTS AND OEICs

The same general principles apply as to unit trusts.

GOVERNMENT STOCKS (GILT EDGED)

Risk profile
Extremely low risk. The whole fabric of society would have to crumble to have any risk exposure.

Income
Fixed income. No chance of increasing income.

Capital protection
Little chance of capital appreciation, except with index linked stocks.

Tax breaks
Profits on sale not liable to capital gains tax.

Simplicity
Easy to understand.

NATIONAL SAVINGS

Risk profile
All National Savings are extremely low risk. They are government backed.

NSB accounts
Income
Fixed interest. Low rates of interest.

Capital protection
None. The money in the bank gets no capital appreciation.

Tax breaks
The first £70 per year of ordinary account interest is exempt from tax.

Simplicity
Extremely simple to understand and operate.

National Savings Certificates (fixed interest)
Income
No income during the five year term. All income is rolled up. Penalty for early surrender.

Capital protection
None. The capital stays fixed.

Tax breaks
The interest is exempt from income tax.

Simplicity
Easy to understand and operate. A lump sum is invested, then withdrawn five years later.

National Savings Certificates (index linked)
Income
No income during the five year term. All interest is rolled up. Interest at lower rate than ordinary certificates. Penalty for early surrender.

Capital protection
The capital is protected from inflation.

Tax breaks
The interest and inflation addition is exempt from income tax.

PENSION FUNDS

Risk profile
Low risk. Long term investment. Capital is locked up until retirement.

Income
None until retirement benefits are taken.

Capital protection
Excellent. The tax advantages can make this the best long term low risk investment.

Tax breaks
Full tax relief on premiums paid. A tax free lump sum available when benefits are taken.

Simplicity
Easy to understand – pay in while you work, take out when you retire.

PROPERTY

Risk profile
Low risk in the long term – but be sure to get a full survey to ensure the property is sound.

Income
Reasonable income with prospects of increasing the income in time.

Capital protection
Good in the long term – but can be liable to extreme fluctuation in the short term.

Tax breaks
Holiday letting income qualifies as earned income – otherwise no tax breaks.

Simplicity
Easy to understand, but make sure that all the technical aspects are taken care of by professionals.

HOME INCOME PLANS

Risk profile
You must make sure of safeguards to protect your home.

Income
Depends on type of plan.

Capital protection
Depends on the type of investment. If linked to an annuity, there is no capital protection.

Tax breaks
None.

Simplicity
Easy to understand. Releasing the value tied up in your house provides extra income. But the details must be vetted to ensure absolute security for your home.

LIFE ASSURANCE

Risk profile
Low risk, especially if the policy is 'with profits'.

Income
Only income bonds can produce an income.

Capital protection
In general, not the best vehicle for long term capital protection.

Tax breaks
Some situations can benefit from bonds.

Simplicity
Easy to understand.

ETHICAL INVESTMENTS

These do not fit into a category for risk, income, capital protection or simplicity.

COLLECTIBLES

Risk profile
Can be high – there might not be a large market. There may be a physical risk to the collection.

Income
No income generated unless you actively trade.

Capital protection
Variable. Can be good, but at the mercy of sentiment. Collectibles can easily go out of fashion.

Tax breaks
None.

COMMODITIES

Risk profile
High.

Income
None. Depends on making capital profits.

Capital protection
Can be extremely good, or extremely bad.

Tax breaks
None.

Simplicity
Not easy to understand.

PLAYING THE MARKET

Risk profile
High.

Income
None. Depends on capital profits.

Capital protection
Can be very good, or very bad.

Tax breaks
None.

Simplicity
In theory, very easy. In practice, you need to keep abreast of market prices, rumours, *etc.*

DERIVATIVES

Risk profile
Medium to high.

Income
None. Depends on capital profits.

Capital protection
Low.

Tax Breaks
None.

Simplicity
Not easy to understand.

SPREAD BETTING

Risk profile
Extremely high.

Income
None.

Capital protection
None.

Tax breaks
None.

Simplicity
Not easy to understand.

BANK AND BUILDING SOCIETY ACCOUNTS

Risk profile
Low.

Income
Fixed interest – usually quite low. Variable.

Capital protection
None.

Tax breaks
TESSAs and ISAs available.

Simplicity
Very easy to understand and operate.

Appendix 2
The Twelve Commandments
of Saving and Investing

1. Keep it simple.

2. You cannot buck the market, so do not try to.

3. If something seems too good to be true, it probably is.

4. There is no reward without the risk.

5. You cannot have too much information.

6. Do not try to live off your capital.

7. Do not put all your eggs in one basket.

8. You are never too young to start saving.

9. Do not let the incentive tail wag the investment dog.

10. If you do not understand it, do not invest in it.

11. Ethical investments are not necessarily low risk.

12. Never let yourself be rushed or pressured into an investment.

Glossary

AIM. Alternative Investment Market: a market for shares in public companies not yet quoted on the Stock Exchange.

AVC. Additional Voluntary Contributions: additional contributions which may be made by employees to their superannuation scheme.

Blue chips. The term given to the best quality equity investments.

Bonds. Many investments use this term. It can be a National Savings product, a single premium life assurance policy, or a building society product.

Churning. The practice by which brokers change investments more than necessary to generate commission for themselves.

Commodities. Goods used in trading which can be used as a speculative investment.

Commission. The remuneration given to intermediaries by the company issuing the investment or policy, usually as a percentage of the amount invested.

Dividends. The return given to shareholders in a company, as their share of the profits of that company.

Endowment policy. A type of life assurance which entitles the insured person to a lump sum on attaining a certain age.

Equities. Investments in the ordinary shares of companies.

Ethical investments. Investments that promote, either positively or negatively, a set of values which the investor wishes to uphold.

Gilt edged. A government backed stock.

Home income plan. One of several types of plans which release the capital locked up in a house to give income to the owner.

Income drawdown. Provisions by which a person may delay taking the full benefits from their pension fund, but draw 'income' from the fund in the meantime.

Income multiplier. The measure of how much mortgage a lender will give by reference to the income of the borrower.

Index tracker funds. Collective investments which invest in the shares making up the index it is 'tracking'. It therefore requires less management than a conventional collective investment.

Independent adviser. An adviser who is registered and can give advice on a range of products.

Inheritance tax. Tax charged on a person's estate which passes to his survivors on death.

Investment trust. A quoted company which invests in the shares of other companies.

ISA. Individual Savings Account: a form of tax exempt savings and investment.

Life assurance. A contract between an insurer and an individual under which the insurer pays out a sum on the death of the insured person.

Market sectors. The different commercial activities represented by the shares quoted on the Stock Exchange.

Mortgage. A loan which is secured on a house or other property.

OEIC. Open Ended Investment Company: a company which invests in other companies. It shares some of the characteristics of investment trusts, and some characteristics of unit trusts.

Options. The right to trade in investments at a future date at a predetermined price.

Ordinary shares. Shares in a company which give the owner full profit sharing rights.

PEP. Personal Equity Plan: a form of tax exempt investment.

Personal pension. A government approved scheme for self-employed or employed people without a superannuation scheme to provide for their pension. It enjoys tax relief.

Portfolio. A list of your investments and savings of all sorts. Can be applied more restrictively to the list of your shares.

Potentially exempt transfer. A transfer from one person to another which is exempt from inheritance tax if the donor survives seven years.

Preference shares. Shares in a company which have a preferential repayment right in the case of liquidation, but usually only pay interest, not dividends.

Redemption. The repayment of a loan or obligation.

SERPS. State Earnings Related Pension Scheme: the pension for employed people paying earnings related National Insurance.

Shareholder concessions. Goods or services of the company given to shareholders at specially discounted rates.

Shares. The unit of ownership of a company.

Spread betting. A form of gambling on the future outcome of some event, sometimes used as a hedge against investment losses.

Stock broker. The intermediary through whom you can deal on the Stock Exchange.

Stock exchange. The place where stocks and share are bought and sold. The principal exchange in this country is the London Stock Exchange.

Superannuation scheme. Scheme for employees of a company to provide for their retirement pension.

TEP. Traded Endowment Policy: an endowment policy which the original person has sold. A new person takes over the benefits and obligations of the policy.

TESSA. Tax Exempt Special Savings Account: a form of tax exempt savings.

Tied agent. An adviser who is 'tied' to one company and can only sell their products.

Tracker funds. See Index tracker funds.

Trusts. A legal device by which a person puts money into the care of trustees to be used for the benefit of others as the donor decides.

Unit trusts. A collective investment in which individual investors pay into a fund which the managers invest in a wide range of stocks and shares.

USM. Unlisted Securities Market: an alternative market for buying and selling shares of smaller companies not yet quoted on the Stock Exchange or the AIM.

Warrants. Instruments giving the right to buy shares in a company at a future date at a fixed price.

Yield. The actual annual rate of return or interest you will get by investing in an investment at the price quoted.

Summary of Case Studies

Alison

Alison earned £15,000 per year when she started saving for a deposit on a house and her fiancé earned £12,000 per year. At the end of two years, she was earning £18,000 per year, and her fiancé was earning £15,000 per year. By that time they had saved £8,000 which they used as a deposit on a house. They were then each aged 25. They got married at the same time, and took out a mortgage for £40,000. They opted for an interest only mortgage and paid interest only of £300 per month. Her husband paid £100 per month in pension premiums, and she paid a similar amount into an endowment policy. In addition, they each put away £25 per month to a regular savings account. Alison also has the small National Savings account and a few Premium Bonds.

They have started their married life with a good regular savings habit.

Brian

Brian is in his late forties and earns £35,000 per year. His wife has also recently taken a part time job and earns £6,000 per year. Brian's main concern is providing for his retirement, and he puts in the maximum contribution to his firm's pension scheme. In addition he puts in the maximum to a free standing AVC scheme (Additional Voluntary Contributions). He has received a legacy of £5,000 and put this into an ISA. His wife also saves a little from her earnings — in the form of regular investments into an ISA.

Brian and his wife also make wills, leaving everything to each other, and then to the children, or any grandchildren they may have in the future.

Charles

Charles has just retired with a company pension and a lump sum of £20,000. He also has an endowment policy maturing for £40,000. Later, he obtains a shared appreciation mortgage of £20,000.

He has a National Insurance Pension, and the company pension, which together come to about £10,000 per year. He puts £10,000 into

Pensioners Guaranteed Income Bonds – a National Savings product. He invests £30,000 in a portfolio of stocks and shares recommended by a stockbroker. He also puts £20,000 in unit trusts. A further £5,000 is invested in small companies ("penny shares"). He has a total of £15,000 in a few building society accounts.

He feels that he has gone about his affairs in a piecemeal way, and goes to see a financial adviser (see Chapter 14). He sees the adviser with his wife, and then changes his investments to put some in his wife's name. This equalises the income more, and is more tax efficient. He also puts some of the investments into ISAs, and gets rid of his penny shares. He finishes up with this profile:

Capital

	Charles	**His wife**
ISAs	£6,000	£6,000
Life assurance bonds	£10,000	£20,000
Unit trusts		£20,000
Shares		£10,000
Building Society account	£4,000	£4,000

Income

Pensions	£10,000	
ISAs	£300	£300
Life Assurance Bonds	£500	£1,000
Unit trusts		£1,000
Shares		£400
Building Society interest	£200	£200
Total Incomes	£11,000	£2,600

Further Reading

Books

Managing Your Personal Finances by John Claxton – How To Books
Coping with Self Assessment by John Whiteley – How To Books
Investing in Stocks and Shares by Dr John White – How To Books
Personal Finance on the Net by John Whiteley – How To Books
Investment Made Easy by Jim Slater – Orion Books
The Zulu Principle by Jim Slater – Orion Books
The Instant Investor by E. B. Groves – Charles Letts
The Warren Buffet Way: Investment Strategies of the World's Greatest Investor by Robert G. Hagstrom – John Wiley
The Online Investor by Peter Temple – John Wiley
Soros on Soros: Staying Ahead of the Curve by George Soros – John Wiley
How to Choose Stockmarket Winners by Raymond Caley – Piatkus
Investors Chronicle Good Peps Guide by Debbie Harrison – Pitman
Traded Options by Brian Millard – John Wiley
Understand Bonds and Gilts in a Day by Ian Bruce – Take That
The Ethical Investor by Russell Sparkes – Harper Collins
Elliott Wave Principle by A. J. Frost and R. R. Prechter – New Classics Library

Periodicals

Financial Times
Investors Chronicle

Useful Addresses

Building Societies Association, 3 Saville Row, London W1.

Council of Mortgage Lenders, 3 Saville Row, London W1.

The London Metal Exchange Ltd, 56 Leadenhall Street, London EC3A 2BJ.

The Baltic Exchange, St Mary Axe, London EC3A 8BH.

Ethical Investment Research Service (EIRIS), 504 Bondway Business Centre, 71 Bondway, London SW8 1SQ.

London International Financial Futures Exchange, Cousin Lane, Canon Bridge, London EC4.

Age Concern, Astral House, 1268 London Road, London SW16 4ER.

Association of Investment Trust Companies, Durrant House, 8–13 Chiswell Street, London EC1Y 4YY.

Association of Policy Market Makers, Holywell Centre, Phipp Street, London EC2.

National Savings Sales Information Unit, Freepost BJ2092, Blackpool FY3 9XR.

National Savings Bank, Glasgow G58 1BR.

National Savings Certificates, Durham DH99 1BR.

Spread betting

City Index Ltd, Cardinal Court, 23 St Thomas More Street, London E1 9YY.

IG Index PLC, 1 Warwick Row, London SW1E 5ER.

Stock Exchange

Public Information Department, London Stock Exchange, London EC2N 1HP.

Association of Unit Trust and Investment Funds, 65 Kingsway, London WC2.

Index